C-3875

CAREER EXAMINATION SERIES

THIS IS YOUR **PASSBOOK**® FOR ...

CONSTRUCTION & SKILLED TRADES SELECTION TEST (CAST)

NLC®

NATIONAL LEARNING CORPORATION®
passbooks.com

PASSBOOK® SERIES

THE *PASSBOOK® SERIES* has been created to prepare applicants and candidates for the ultimate academic battlefield – the examination room.

At some time in our lives, each and every one of us may be required to take an examination – for validation, matriculation, admission, qualification, registration, certification, or licensure.

Based on the assumption that every applicant or candidate has met the basic formal educational standards, has taken the required number of courses, and read the necessary texts, the *PASSBOOK® SERIES* furnishes the one special preparation which may assure passing with confidence, instead of failing with insecurity. Examination questions – together with answers – are furnished as the basic vehicle for study so that the mysteries of the examination and its compounding difficulties may be eliminated or diminished by a sure method.

This book is meant to help you pass your examination provided that you qualify and are serious in your objective.

The entire field is reviewed through the huge store of content information which is succinctly presented through a provocative and challenging approach – the question-and-answer method.

A climate of success is established by furnishing the correct answers at the end of each test.

You soon learn to recognize types of questions, forms of questions, and patterns of questioning. You may even begin to anticipate expected outcomes.

You perceive that many questions are repeated or adapted so that you can gain acute insights, which may enable you to score many sure points.

You learn how to confront new questions, or types of questions, and to attack them confidently and work out the correct answers.

You note objectives and emphases, and recognize pitfalls and dangers, so that you may make positive educational adjustments.

Moreover, you are kept fully informed in relation to new concepts, methods, practices, and directions in the field.

You discover that you arre actually taking the examination all the time: you are preparing for the examination by "taking" an examination, not by reading extraneous and/or supererogatory textbooks.

In short, this PASSBOOK®, used directedly, should be an important factor in helping you to pass your test.

CONSTRUCTION AND SKILLED TRADES
SELECTION TEST
(CAST)

CAST is a battery of aptitude tests designed and validated to aid in the selection of candidates across a wide variety of construction and skilled trades occupations. CAST is a comprehensive battery of paper-and-pencil tests which can predict candidates' probability of success in the following categories of construction and skilled trade jobs:

1. Transmission and distribution
2. Facilities and repair
3. Other facilities (e.g., carpenter)
4. Electrical repair
5. Machining and vehicle repair
6. Meter service and repair

A description of the four aptitude tests comprising the CAST battery is provided below:

I.   **Graphic Arithmetic**
      This test measures a candidate's ability to solve arithmetic problems by using information from prints or drawings. The test contains two drawings, each followed by several questions. The test has 16 questions and a 30-minute time limit.

      Examples:

Use the drawing shown below to answer the two example questions. (Please note that the dimensions shown on the drawing are not necessarily drawn exactly to scale.)

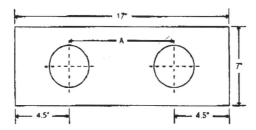

1. What is the distance "A" between the centers of the two holes?

         A) 6.0"
         B) 7.0"
         C) 8.0"
         D) 12.5"
         E) None of these

2. What was the surface area of the side shown in the drawing before the holes were drilled?

     A) 24.0 square inches
     B) 79.0 square inches
     C) 84.0 square inches
     D) 109.0 square inches
     E) None of these

II.   Mechanical Concepts

This test measures a candidate's ability to understand mechanical principles. There are 44 multiple-choice items. Each item contains a pictorial description of a mechanical situation, a question and three possible answers. The test has a 20-minute time limit.

Examples:

3. In the figure below, at which point should pressurized air enter the cylinder to lower the piston? (If both, mark C)

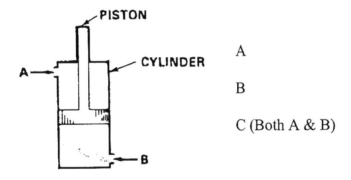

A

B

C (Both A & B)

4. To keep the beam horizontal when lifted, at which point should you hook the cable?

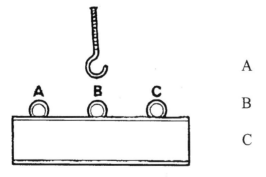

A

B

C

III.   Reading for Comprehension

This test measures a candidate's ability to read and understand written materials. The test consists of four reading passages, each followed by several multiple-choice questions about the passage. There are 32 items and a 30-minute time limit on this test.

IV.   Mathematical Usage

This test measures a candidate's ability to work with mathematical formulas. It consists of 18 multiple-choice items and has a 7-minute time limit.

Example:

5. 2 quarts = ? gallons

A) .4
B) 2
C) .5
D) 5
E) None of these

Scoring Procedure

The four aptitude test scores are combined to form a single Index Score, ranging from 1 to 10. Candidates' index scores are then translated into expected probabilities of successful job performance.

A candidate's standing on this overall index score should be interpreted as a measure of ability to learn and perform the job. Candidates with high index scores should be expected to understand mathematical relationships, perceive details quickly and accurately, and possess effective reasoning skills.

———

KEY (CORRECT ANSWERS)

1. C 2. E 3. A 4. B 5. C

———

HOW TO TAKE A TEST

I. YOU MUST PASS AN EXAMINATION

A. *WHAT EVERY CANDIDATE SHOULD KNOW*

Examination applicants often ask us for help in preparing for the written test. What can I study in advance? What kinds of questions will be asked? How will the test be given? How will the papers be graded?

As an applicant for a civil service examination, you may be wondering about some of these things. Our purpose here is to suggest effective methods of advance study and to describe civil service examinations.

Your chances for success on this examination can be increased if you know how to prepare. Those "pre-examination jitters" can be reduced if you know what to expect. You can even experience an adventure in good citizenship if you know why civil service exams are given.

B. *WHY ARE CIVIL SERVICE EXAMINATIONS GIVEN?*

Civil service examinations are important to you in two ways. As a citizen, you want public jobs filled by employees who know how to do their work. As a job seeker, you want a fair chance to compete for that job on an equal footing with other candidates. The best-known means of accomplishing this two-fold goal is the competitive examination.

Exams are widely publicized throughout the nation. They may be administered for jobs in federal, state, city, municipal, town or village governments or agencies.

Any citizen may apply, with some limitations, such as the age or residence of applicants. Your experience and education may be reviewed to see whether you meet the requirements for the particular examination. When these requirements exist, they are reasonable and applied consistently to all applicants. Thus, a competitive examination may cause you some uneasiness now, but it is your privilege and safeguard.

C. *HOW ARE CIVIL SERVICE EXAMS DEVELOPED?*

Examinations are carefully written by trained technicians who are specialists in the field known as "psychological measurement," in consultation with recognized authorities in the field of work that the test will cover. These experts recommend the subject matter areas or skills to be tested; only those knowledges or skills important to your success on the job are included. The most reliable books and source materials available are used as references. Together, the experts and technicians judge the difficulty level of the questions.

Test technicians know how to phrase questions so that the problem is clearly stated. Their ethics do not permit "trick" or "catch" questions. Questions may have been tried out on sample groups, or subjected to statistical analysis, to determine their usefulness.

Written tests are often used in combination with performance tests, ratings of training and experience, and oral interviews. All of these measures combine to form the best-known means of finding the right person for the right job.

II. HOW TO PASS THE WRITTEN TEST

A. NATURE OF THE EXAMINATION

To prepare intelligently for civil service examinations, you should know how they differ from school examinations you have taken. In school you were assigned certain definite pages to read or subjects to cover. The examination questions were quite detailed and usually emphasized memory. Civil service exams, on the other hand, try to discover your present ability to perform the duties of a position, plus your potentiality to learn these duties. In other words, a civil service exam attempts to predict how successful you will be. Questions cover such a broad area that they cannot be as minute and detailed as school exam questions.

In the public service similar kinds of work, or positions, are grouped together in one "class." This process is known as *position-classification*. All the positions in a class are paid according to the salary range for that class. One class title covers all of these positions, and they are all tested by the same examination.

B. FOUR BASIC STEPS

1) Study the announcement

How, then, can you know what subjects to study? Our best answer is: "Learn as much as possible about the class of positions for which you've applied." The exam will test the knowledge, skills and abilities needed to do the work.

Your most valuable source of information about the position you want is the official exam announcement. This announcement lists the training and experience qualifications. Check these standards and apply only if you come reasonably close to meeting them.

The brief description of the position in the examination announcement offers some clues to the subjects which will be tested. Think about the job itself. Review the duties in your mind. Can you perform them, or are there some in which you are rusty? Fill in the blank spots in your preparation.

Many jurisdictions preview the written test in the exam announcement by including a section called "Knowledge and Abilities Required," "Scope of the Examination," or some similar heading. Here you will find out specifically what fields will be tested.

2) Review your own background

Once you learn in general what the position is all about, and what you need to know to do the work, ask yourself which subjects you already know fairly well and which need improvement. You may wonder whether to concentrate on improving your strong areas or on building some background in your fields of weakness. When the announcement has specified "some knowledge" or "considerable knowledge," or has used adjectives like "beginning principles of…" or "advanced … methods," you can get a clue as to the number and difficulty of questions to be asked in any given field. More questions, and hence broader coverage, would be included for those subjects which are more important in the work. Now weigh your strengths and weaknesses against the job requirements and prepare accordingly.

3) Determine the level of the position

Another way to tell how intensively you should prepare is to understand the level of the job for which you are applying. Is it the entering level? In other words, is this the position in which beginners in a field of work are hired? Or is it an intermediate or advanced level? Sometimes this is indicated by such words as "Junior" or "Senior" in the class title. Other jurisdictions use Roman numerals to designate the level – Clerk I, Clerk II, for example. The word "Supervisor" sometimes appears in the title. If the level is not indicated by the title, check the description of duties. Will you be working under very close supervision, or will you have responsibility for independent decisions in this work?

4) Choose appropriate study materials

Now that you know the subjects to be examined and the relative amount of each subject to be covered, you can choose suitable study materials. For beginning level jobs, or even advanced ones, if you have a pronounced weakness in some aspect of your training, read a modern, standard textbook in that field. Be sure it is up to date and has general coverage. Such books are normally available at your library, and the librarian will be glad to help you locate one. For entry-level positions, questions of appropriate difficulty are chosen – neither highly advanced questions, nor those too simple. Such questions require careful thought but not advanced training.

If the position for which you are applying is technical or advanced, you will read more advanced, specialized material. If you are already familiar with the basic principles of your field, elementary textbooks would waste your time. Concentrate on advanced textbooks and technical periodicals. Think through the concepts and review difficult problems in your field.

These are all general sources. You can get more ideas on your own initiative, following these leads. For example, training manuals and publications of the government agency which employs workers in your field can be useful, particularly for technical and professional positions. A letter or visit to the government department involved may result in more specific study suggestions, and certainly will provide you with a more definite idea of the exact nature of the position you are seeking.

III. KINDS OF TESTS

Tests are used for purposes other than measuring knowledge and ability to perform specified duties. For some positions, it is equally important to test ability to make adjustments to new situations or to profit from training. In others, basic mental abilities not dependent on information are essential. Questions which test these things may not appear as pertinent to the duties of the position as those which test for knowledge and information. Yet they are often highly important parts of a fair examination. For very general questions, it is almost impossible to help you direct your study efforts. What we can do is to point out some of the more common of these general abilities needed in public service positions and describe some typical questions.

1) General information

Broad, general information has been found useful for predicting job success in some kinds of work. This is tested in a variety of ways, from vocabulary lists to questions about current events. Basic background in some field of work, such as sociology or economics, may be sampled in a group of questions. Often these are principles which have become familiar to most persons through exposure rather than through formal training. It is difficult to advise you how to study for these questions; being alert to the world around you is our best suggestion.

2) Verbal ability

An example of an ability needed in many positions is verbal or language ability. Verbal ability is, in brief, the ability to use and understand words. Vocabulary and grammar tests are typical measures of this ability. Reading comprehension or paragraph interpretation questions are common in many kinds of civil service tests. You are given a paragraph of written material and asked to find its central meaning.

3) Numerical ability

Number skills can be tested by the familiar arithmetic problem, by checking paired lists of numbers to see which are alike and which are different, or by interpreting charts and graphs. In the latter test, a graph may be printed in the test booklet which you are asked to use as the basis for answering questions.

4) Observation

A popular test for law-enforcement positions is the observation test. A picture is shown to you for several minutes, then taken away. Questions about the picture test your ability to observe both details and larger elements.

5) Following directions

In many positions in the public service, the employee must be able to carry out written instructions dependably and accurately. You may be given a chart with several columns, each column listing a variety of information. The questions require you to carry out directions involving the information given in the chart.

6) Skills and aptitudes

Performance tests effectively measure some manual skills and aptitudes. When the skill is one in which you are trained, such as typing or shorthand, you can practice. These tests are often very much like those given in business school or high school courses. For many of the other skills and aptitudes, however, no short-time preparation can be made. Skills and abilities natural to you or that you have developed throughout your lifetime are being tested.

Many of the general questions just described provide all the data needed to answer the questions and ask you to use your reasoning ability to find the answers. Your best preparation for these tests, as well as for tests of facts and ideas, is to be at your physical and mental best. You, no doubt, have your own methods of getting into an exam-taking mood and keeping "in shape." The next section lists some ideas on this subject.

IV. KINDS OF QUESTIONS

Only rarely is the "essay" question, which you answer in narrative form, used in civil service tests. Civil service tests are usually of the short-answer type. Full instructions for answering these questions will be given to you at the examination. But in case this is your first experience with short-answer questions and separate answer sheets, here is what you need to know:

1) Multiple-choice Questions

Most popular of the short-answer questions is the "multiple choice" or "best answer" question. It can be used, for example, to test for factual knowledge, ability to solve problems or judgment in meeting situations found at work.

A multiple-choice question is normally one of three types—

- It can begin with an incomplete statement followed by several possible endings. You are to find the one ending which *best* completes the statement, although some of the others may not be entirely wrong.
- It can also be a complete statement in the form of a question which is answered by choosing one of the statements listed.
- It can be in the form of a problem – again you select the best answer.

Here is an example of a multiple-choice question with a discussion which should give you some clues as to the method for choosing the right answer:

When an employee has a complaint about his assignment, the action which will *best* help him overcome his difficulty is to
- A. discuss his difficulty with his coworkers
- B. take the problem to the head of the organization
- C. take the problem to the person who gave him the assignment
- D. say nothing to anyone about his complaint

In answering this question, you should study each of the choices to find which is best. Consider choice "A" – Certainly an employee may discuss his complaint with fellow employees, but no change or improvement can result, and the complaint remains unresolved. Choice "B" is a poor choice since the head of the organization probably does not know what assignment you have been given, and taking your problem to him is known as "going over the head" of the supervisor. The supervisor, or person who made the assignment, is the person who can clarify it or correct any injustice. Choice "C" is, therefore, correct. To say nothing, as in choice "D," is unwise. Supervisors have and interest in knowing the problems employees are facing, and the employee is seeking a solution to his problem.

2) True/False Questions

The "true/false" or "right/wrong" form of question is sometimes used. Here a complete statement is given. Your job is to decide whether the statement is right or wrong.

SAMPLE: A roaming cell-phone call to a nearby city costs less than a non-roaming call to a distant city.

This statement is wrong, or false, since roaming calls are more expensive.

This is not a complete list of all possible question forms, although most of the others are variations of these common types. You will always get complete directions for answering questions. Be sure you understand *how* to mark your answers – ask questions until you do.

V. RECORDING YOUR ANSWERS

Computer terminals are used more and more today for many different kinds of exams.

For an examination with very few applicants, you may be told to record your answers in the test booklet itself. Separate answer sheets are much more common. If this separate answer sheet is to be scored by machine – and this is often the case – it is highly important that you mark your answers correctly in order to get credit.

An electronic scoring machine is often used in civil service offices because of the speed with which papers can be scored. Machine-scored answer sheets must be marked with a pencil, which will be given to you. This pencil has a high graphite content which responds to the electronic scoring machine. As a matter of fact, stray dots may register as answers, so do not let your pencil rest on the answer sheet while you are pondering the correct answer. Also, if your pencil lead breaks or is otherwise defective, ask for another.

Since the answer sheet will be dropped in a slot in the scoring machine, be careful not to bend the corners or get the paper crumpled.

The answer sheet normally has five vertical columns of numbers, with 30 numbers to a column. These numbers correspond to the question numbers in your test booklet. After each number, going across the page are four or five pairs of dotted lines. These short dotted lines have small letters or numbers above them. The first two pairs may also have a "T" or "F" above the letters. This indicates that the first two pairs only are to be used if the questions are of the true-false type. If the questions are multiple choice, disregard the "T" and "F" and pay attention only to the small letters or numbers.

Answer your questions in the manner of the sample that follows:

32. The largest city in the United States is
    A. Washington, D.C.
    B. New York City
    C. Chicago
    D. Detroit
    E. San Francisco

1) Choose the answer you think is best. (New York City is the largest, so "B" is correct.)
2) Find the row of dotted lines numbered the same as the question you are answering. (Find row number 32)
3) Find the pair of dotted lines corresponding to the answer. (Find the pair of lines under the mark "B.")
4) Make a solid black mark between the dotted lines.

VI. BEFORE THE TEST

Common sense will help you find procedures to follow to get ready for an examination. Too many of us, however, overlook these sensible measures. Indeed, nervousness and fatigue have been found to be the most serious reasons why applicants fail to do their best on civil service tests. Here is a list of reminders:

- Begin your preparation early – Don't wait until the last minute to go scurrying around for books and materials or to find out what the position is all about.
- Prepare continuously – An hour a night for a week is better than an all-night cram session. This has been definitely established. What is more, a night a week for a month will return better dividends than crowding your study into a shorter period of time.
- Locate the place of the exam – You have been sent a notice telling you when and where to report for the examination. If the location is in a different town or otherwise unfamiliar to you, it would be well to inquire the best route and learn something about the building.
- Relax the night before the test – Allow your mind to rest. Do not study at all that night. Plan some mild recreation or diversion; then go to bed early and get a good night's sleep.
- Get up early enough to make a leisurely trip to the place for the test – This way unforeseen events, traffic snarls, unfamiliar buildings, etc. will not upset you.
- Dress comfortably – A written test is not a fashion show. You will be known by number and not by name, so wear something comfortable.
- Leave excess paraphernalia at home – Shopping bags and odd bundles will get in your way. You need bring only the items mentioned in the official notice you received; usually everything you need is provided. Do not bring reference books to the exam. They will only confuse those last minutes and be taken away from you when in the test room.
- Arrive somewhat ahead of time – If because of transportation schedules you must get there very early, bring a newspaper or magazine to take your mind off yourself while waiting.
- Locate the examination room – When you have found the proper room, you will be directed to the seat or part of the room where you will sit. Sometimes you are given a sheet of instructions to read while you are waiting. Do not fill out any forms until you are told to do so; just read them and be prepared.
- Relax and prepare to listen to the instructions
- If you have any physical problem that may keep you from doing your best, be sure to tell the test administrator. If you are sick or in poor health, you really cannot do your best on the exam. You can come back and take the test some other time.

VII. AT THE TEST

The day of the test is here and you have the test booklet in your hand. The temptation to get going is very strong. Caution! There is more to success than knowing the right answers. You must know how to identify your papers and understand variations in the type of short-answer question used in this particular examination. Follow these suggestions for maximum results from your efforts:

1) Cooperate with the monitor

The test administrator has a duty to create a situation in which you can be as much at ease as possible. He will give instructions, tell you when to begin, check to see that you are marking your answer sheet correctly, and so on. He is not there to guard you, although he will see that your competitors do not take unfair advantage. He wants to help you do your best.

2) Listen to all instructions

Don't jump the gun! Wait until you understand all directions. In most civil service tests you get more time than you need to answer the questions. So don't be in a hurry. Read each word of instructions until you clearly understand the meaning. Study the examples, listen to all announcements and follow directions. Ask questions if you do not understand what to do.

3) Identify your papers

Civil service exams are usually identified by number only. You will be assigned a number; you must not put your name on your test papers. Be sure to copy your number correctly. Since more than one exam may be given, copy your exact examination title.

4) Plan your time

Unless you are told that a test is a "speed" or "rate of work" test, speed itself is usually not important. Time enough to answer all the questions will be provided, but this does not mean that you have all day. An overall time limit has been set. Divide the total time (in minutes) by the number of questions to determine the approximate time you have for each question.

5) Do not linger over difficult questions

If you come across a difficult question, mark it with a paper clip (useful to have along) and come back to it when you have been through the booklet. One caution if you do this – be sure to skip a number on your answer sheet as well. Check often to be sure that you have not lost your place and that you are marking in the row numbered the same as the question you are answering.

6) Read the questions

Be sure you know what the question asks! Many capable people are unsuccessful because they failed to *read* the questions correctly.

7) Answer all questions

Unless you have been instructed that a penalty will be deducted for incorrect answers, it is better to guess than to omit a question.

8) Speed tests

It is often better NOT to guess on speed tests. It has been found that on timed tests people are tempted to spend the last few seconds before time is called in marking answers at random – without even reading them – in the hope of picking up a few extra points. To discourage this practice, the instructions may warn you that your score will be "corrected" for guessing. That is, a penalty will be applied. The incorrect answers will be deducted from the correct ones, or some other penalty formula will be used.

9) Review your answers

If you finish before time is called, go back to the questions you guessed or omitted to give them further thought. Review other answers if you have time.

10) Return your test materials

If you are ready to leave before others have finished or time is called, take ALL your materials to the monitor and leave quietly. Never take any test material with you. The monitor can discover whose papers are not complete, and taking a test booklet may be grounds for disqualification.

VIII. EXAMINATION TECHNIQUES

1) Read the general instructions carefully. These are usually printed on the first page of the exam booklet. As a rule, these instructions refer to the timing of the examination; the fact that you should not start work until the signal and must stop work at a signal, etc. If there are any *special* instructions, such as a choice of questions to be answered, make sure that you note this instruction carefully.

2) When you are ready to start work on the examination, that is as soon as the signal has been given, read the instructions to each question booklet, underline any key words or phrases, such as *least, best, outline, describe* and the like. In this way you will tend to answer as requested rather than discover on reviewing your paper that you *listed without describing*, that you selected the *worst* choice rather than the *best* choice, etc.

3) If the examination is of the objective or multiple-choice type – that is, each question will also give a series of possible answers: A, B, C or D, and you are called upon to select the best answer and write the letter next to that answer on your answer paper – it is advisable to start answering each question in turn. There may be anywhere from 50 to 100 such questions in the three or four hours allotted and you can see how much time would be taken if you read through all the questions before beginning to answer any. Furthermore, if you come across a question or group of questions which you know would be difficult to answer, it would undoubtedly affect your handling of all the other questions.

4) If the examination is of the essay type and contains but a few questions, it is a moot point as to whether you should read all the questions before starting to answer any one. Of course, if you are given a choice – say five out of seven and the like – then it is essential to read all the questions so you can eliminate the two that are most difficult. If, however, you are asked to answer all the questions, there may be danger in trying to answer the easiest one first because you may find that you will spend too much time on it. The best technique is to answer the first question, then proceed to the second, etc.

5) Time your answers. Before the exam begins, write down the time it started, then add the time allowed for the examination and write down the time it must be completed, then divide the time available somewhat as follows:

- If 3-1/2 hours are allowed, that would be 210 minutes. If you have 80 objective-type questions, that would be an average of 2-1/2 minutes per question. Allow yourself no more than 2 minutes per question, or a total of 160 minutes, which will permit about 50 minutes to review.
- If for the time allotment of 210 minutes there are 7 essay questions to answer, that would average about 30 minutes a question. Give yourself only 25 minutes per question so that you have about 35 minutes to review.

6) The most important instruction is to *read each question* and make sure you know what is wanted. The second most important instruction is to *time yourself properly* so that you answer every question. The third most important instruction is to *answer every question*. Guess if you have to but include something for each question. Remember that you will receive no credit for a blank and will probably receive some credit if you write something in answer to an essay question. If you guess a letter – say "B" for a multiple-choice question – you may have guessed right. If you leave a blank as an answer to a multiple-choice question, the examiners may respect your feelings but it will not add a point to your score. Some exams may penalize you for wrong answers, so in such cases *only*, you may not want to guess unless you have some basis for your answer.

7) Suggestions
   a. Objective-type questions
      1. Examine the question booklet for proper sequence of pages and questions
      2. Read all instructions carefully
      3. Skip any question which seems too difficult; return to it after all other questions have been answered
      4. Apportion your time properly; do not spend too much time on any single question or group of questions
      5. Note and underline key words – *all, most, fewest, least, best, worst, same, opposite,* etc.
      6. Pay particular attention to negatives
      7. Note unusual option, e.g., unduly long, short, complex, different or similar in content to the body of the question
      8. Observe the use of "hedging" words – *probably, may, most likely,* etc.
      9. Make sure that your answer is put next to the same number as the question
      10. Do not second-guess unless you have good reason to believe the second answer is definitely more correct
      11. Cross out original answer if you decide another answer is more accurate; do not erase until you are ready to hand your paper in
      12. Answer all questions; guess unless instructed otherwise
      13. Leave time for review

   b. Essay questions
      1. Read each question carefully
      2. Determine exactly what is wanted. Underline key words or phrases.
      3. Decide on outline or paragraph answer

4. Include many different points and elements unless asked to develop any one or two points or elements
5. Show impartiality by giving pros and cons unless directed to select one side only
6. Make and write down any assumptions you find necessary to answer the questions
7. Watch your English, grammar, punctuation and choice of words
8. Time your answers; don't crowd material

8) Answering the essay question

Most essay questions can be answered by framing the specific response around several key words or ideas. Here are a few such key words or ideas:

M's: manpower, materials, methods, money, management
P's: purpose, program, policy, plan, procedure, practice, problems, pitfalls, personnel, public relations

a. Six basic steps in handling problems:
1. Preliminary plan and background development
2. Collect information, data and facts
3. Analyze and interpret information, data and facts
4. Analyze and develop solutions as well as make recommendations
5. Prepare report and sell recommendations
6. Install recommendations and follow up effectiveness

b. Pitfalls to avoid
1. *Taking things for granted* – A statement of the situation does not necessarily imply that each of the elements is necessarily true; for example, a complaint may be invalid and biased so that all that can be taken for granted is that a complaint has been registered
2. *Considering only one side of a situation* – Wherever possible, indicate several alternatives and then point out the reasons you selected the best one
3. *Failing to indicate follow up* – Whenever your answer indicates action on your part, make certain that you will take proper follow-up action to see how successful your recommendations, procedures or actions turn out to be
4. *Taking too long in answering any single question* – Remember to time your answers properly

IX. AFTER THE TEST

Scoring procedures differ in detail among civil service jurisdictions although the general principles are the same. Whether the papers are hand-scored or graded by machine we have described, they are nearly always graded by number. That is, the person who marks the paper knows only the number – never the name – of the applicant. Not until all the papers have been graded will they be matched with names. If other tests, such as training and experience or oral interview ratings have been given, scores will be combined. Different parts of the examination usually have different weights. For example, the written test might count 60 percent of the final grade, and a rating of training and experience 40 percent. In many jurisdictions, veterans will have a certain number of points added to their grades.

After the final grade has been determined, the names are placed in grade order and an eligible list is established. There are various methods for resolving ties between those who get the same final grade – probably the most common is to place first the name of the person whose application was received first. Job offers are made from the eligible list in the order the names appear on it. You will be notified of your grade and your rank as soon as all these computations have been made. This will be done as rapidly as possible.

People who are found to meet the requirements in the announcement are called "eligibles." Their names are put on a list of eligible candidates. An eligible's chances of getting a job depend on how high he stands on this list and how fast agencies are filling jobs from the list.

When a job is to be filled from a list of eligibles, the agency asks for the names of people on the list of eligibles for that job. When the civil service commission receives this request, it sends to the agency the names of the three people highest on this list. Or, if the job to be filled has specialized requirements, the office sends the agency the names of the top three persons who meet these requirements from the general list.

The appointing officer makes a choice from among the three people whose names were sent to him. If the selected person accepts the appointment, the names of the others are put back on the list to be considered for future openings.

That is the rule in hiring from all kinds of eligible lists, whether they are for typist, carpenter, chemist, or something else. For every vacancy, the appointing officer has his choice of any one of the top three eligibles on the list. This explains why the person whose name is on top of the list sometimes does not get an appointment when some of the persons lower on the list do. If the appointing officer chooses the second or third eligible, the No. 1 eligible does not get a job at once, but stays on the list until he is appointed or the list is terminated.

X. HOW TO PASS THE INTERVIEW TEST

The examination for which you applied requires an oral interview test. You have already taken the written test and you are now being called for the interview test – the final part of the formal examination.

You may think that it is not possible to prepare for an interview test and that there are no procedures to follow during an interview. Our purpose is to point out some things you can do in advance that will help you and some good rules to follow and pitfalls to avoid while you are being interviewed.

What is an interview supposed to test?

The written examination is designed to test the technical knowledge and competence of the candidate; the oral is designed to evaluate intangible qualities, not readily measured otherwise, and to establish a list showing the relative fitness of each candidate – as measured against his competitors – for the position sought. Scoring is not on the basis of "right" and "wrong," but on a sliding scale of values ranging from "not passable" to "outstanding." As a matter of fact, it is possible to achieve a relatively low score without a single "incorrect" answer because of evident weakness in the qualities being measured.

Occasionally, an examination may consist entirely of an oral test – either an individual or a group oral. In such cases, information is sought concerning the technical knowledges and abilities of the candidate, since there has been no written examination for this purpose. More commonly, however, an oral test is used to supplement a written examination.

Who conducts interviews?

The composition of oral boards varies among different jurisdictions. In nearly all, a representative of the personnel department serves as chairman. One of the members of the board may be a representative of the department in which the candidate would work. In some cases, "outside experts" are used, and, frequently, a businessman or some other representative of the general public is asked to serve. Labor and management or other special groups may be represented. The aim is to secure the services of experts in the appropriate field.

However the board is composed, it is a good idea (and not at all improper or unethical) to ascertain in advance of the interview who the members are and what groups they represent. When you are introduced to them, you will have some idea of their backgrounds and interests, and at least you will not stutter and stammer over their names.

What should be done before the interview?

While knowledge about the board members is useful and takes some of the surprise element out of the interview, there is other preparation which is more substantive. It *is* possible to prepare for an oral interview – in several ways:

1) Keep a copy of your application and review it carefully before the interview

This may be the only document before the oral board, and the starting point of the interview. Know what education and experience you have listed there, and the sequence and dates of all of it. Sometimes the board will ask you to review the highlights of your experience for them; you should not have to hem and haw doing it.

2) Study the class specification and the examination announcement

Usually, the oral board has one or both of these to guide them. The qualities, characteristics or knowledges required by the position sought are stated in these documents. They offer valuable clues as to the nature of the oral interview. For example, if the job involves supervisory responsibilities, the announcement will usually indicate that knowledge of modern supervisory methods and the qualifications of the candidate as a supervisor will be tested. If so, you can expect such questions, frequently in the form of a hypothetical situation which you are expected to solve. NEVER go into an oral without knowledge of the duties and responsibilities of the job you seek.

3) Think through each qualification required

Try to visualize the kind of questions you would ask if you were a board member. How well could you answer them? Try especially to appraise your own knowledge and background in each area, *measured against the job sought*, and identify any areas in which you are weak. Be critical and realistic – do not flatter yourself.

4) Do some general reading in areas in which you feel you may be weak

For example, if the job involves supervision and your past experience has NOT, some general reading in supervisory methods and practices, particularly in the field of human relations, might be useful. Do NOT study agency procedures or detailed manuals. The oral board will be testing your understanding and capacity, not your memory.

5) Get a good night's sleep and watch your general health and mental attitude

You will want a clear head at the interview. Take care of a cold or any other minor ailment, and of course, no hangovers.

What should be done on the day of the interview?

Now comes the day of the interview itself. Give yourself plenty of time to get there. Plan to arrive somewhat ahead of the scheduled time, particularly if your appointment is in the fore part of the day. If a previous candidate fails to appear, the board might be ready for you a bit early. By early afternoon an oral board is almost invariably behind schedule if there are many candidates, and you may have to wait. Take along a book or magazine to read, or your application to review, but leave any extraneous material in the waiting room when you go in for your interview. In any event, relax and compose yourself.

The matter of dress is important. The board is forming impressions about you – from your experience, your manners, your attitude, and your appearance. Give your personal appearance careful attention. Dress your best, but not your flashiest. Choose conservative, appropriate clothing, and be sure it is immaculate. This is a business interview, and your appearance should indicate that you regard it as such. Besides, being well groomed and properly dressed will help boost your confidence.

Sooner or later, someone will call your name and escort you into the interview room. *This is it.* From here on you are on your own. It is too late for any more preparation. But remember, you asked for this opportunity to prove your fitness, and you are here because your request was granted.

What happens when you go in?

The usual sequence of events will be as follows: The clerk (who is often the board stenographer) will introduce you to the chairman of the oral board, who will introduce you to the other members of the board. Acknowledge the introductions before you sit down. Do not be surprised if you find a microphone facing you or a stenotypist sitting by. Oral interviews are usually recorded in the event of an appeal or other review.

Usually the chairman of the board will open the interview by reviewing the highlights of your education and work experience from your application – primarily for the benefit of the other members of the board, as well as to get the material into the record. Do not interrupt or comment unless there is an error or significant misinterpretation; if that is the case, do not hesitate. But do not quibble about insignificant matters. Also, he will usually ask you some question about your education, experience or your present job – partly to get you to start talking and to establish the interviewing "rapport." He may start the actual questioning, or turn it over to one of the other members. Frequently, each member undertakes the questioning on a particular area, one in which he is perhaps most competent, so you can expect each member to participate in the examination. Because time is limited, you may also expect some rather abrupt switches in the direction the questioning takes, so do not be upset by it. Normally, a board member will not pursue a single line of questioning unless he discovers a particular strength or weakness.

After each member has participated, the chairman will usually ask whether any member has any further questions, then will ask you if you have anything you wish to add. Unless you are expecting this question, it may floor you. Worse, it may start you off on an extended, extemporaneous speech. The board is not usually seeking more information. The question is principally to offer you a last opportunity to present further qualifications or to indicate that you have nothing to add. So, if you feel that a significant qualification or characteristic has been overlooked, it is proper to point it out in a sentence or so. Do not compliment the board on the thoroughness of their examination – they have been sketchy, and you know it. If you wish, merely say, "No thank you, I have nothing further to add." This is a point where you can "talk yourself out" of a good impression or fail to present an important bit of information. Remember, *you close the interview yourself.*

The chairman will then say, "That is all, Mr. _____, thank you." Do not be startled; the interview is over, and quicker than you think. Thank him, gather your belongings and take your leave. Save your sigh of relief for the other side of the door.

How to put your best foot forward

Throughout this entire process, you may feel that the board individually and collectively is trying to pierce your defenses, seek out your hidden weaknesses and embarrass and confuse you. Actually, this is not true. They are obliged to make an appraisal of your qualifications for the job you are seeking, and they want to see you in your best light. Remember, they must interview all candidates and a non-cooperative candidate may become a failure in spite of their best efforts to bring out his qualifications. Here are 15 suggestions that will help you:

1) Be natural – Keep your attitude confident, not cocky

If you are not confident that you can do the job, do not expect the board to be. Do not apologize for your weaknesses, try to bring out your strong points. The board is interested in a positive, not negative, presentation. Cockiness will antagonize any board member and make him wonder if you are covering up a weakness by a false show of strength.

2) Get comfortable, but don't lounge or sprawl

Sit erectly but not stiffly. A careless posture may lead the board to conclude that you are careless in other things, or at least that you are not impressed by the importance of the occasion. Either conclusion is natural, even if incorrect. Do not fuss with your clothing, a pencil or an ashtray. Your hands may occasionally be useful to emphasize a point; do not let them become a point of distraction.

3) Do not wisecrack or make small talk

This is a serious situation, and your attitude should show that you consider it as such. Further, the time of the board is limited – they do not want to waste it, and neither should you.

4) Do not exaggerate your experience or abilities

In the first place, from information in the application or other interviews and sources, the board may know more about you than you think. Secondly, you probably will not get away with it. An experienced board is rather adept at spotting such a situation, so do not take the chance.

5) If you know a board member, do not make a point of it, yet do not hide it

Certainly you are not fooling him, and probably not the other members of the board. Do not try to take advantage of your acquaintanceship – it will probably do you little good.

6) Do not dominate the interview

Let the board do that. They will give you the clues – do not assume that you have to do all the talking. Realize that the board has a number of questions to ask you, and do not try to take up all the interview time by showing off your extensive knowledge of the answer to the first one.

7) Be attentive

You only have 20 minutes or so, and you should keep your attention at its sharpest throughout. When a member is addressing a problem or question to you, give him your undivided attention. Address your reply principally to him, but do not exclude the other board members.

8) Do not interrupt

A board member may be stating a problem for you to analyze. He will ask you a question when the time comes. Let him state the problem, and wait for the question.

9) Make sure you understand the question

Do not try to answer until you are sure what the question is. If it is not clear, restate it in your own words or ask the board member to clarify it for you. However, do not haggle about minor elements.

10) Reply promptly but not hastily

A common entry on oral board rating sheets is "candidate responded readily," or "candidate hesitated in replies." Respond as promptly and quickly as you can, but do not jump to a hasty, ill-considered answer.

11) Do not be peremptory in your answers

A brief answer is proper – but do not fire your answer back. That is a losing game from your point of view. The board member can probably ask questions much faster than you can answer them.

12) Do not try to create the answer you think the board member wants

He is interested in what kind of mind you have and how it works – not in playing games. Furthermore, he can usually spot this practice and will actually grade you down on it.

13) Do not switch sides in your reply merely to agree with a board member

Frequently, a member will take a contrary position merely to draw you out and to see if you are willing and able to defend your point of view. Do not start a debate, yet do not surrender a good position. If a position is worth taking, it is worth defending.

14) Do not be afraid to admit an error in judgment if you are shown to be wrong

The board knows that you are forced to reply without any opportunity for careful consideration. Your answer may be demonstrably wrong. If so, admit it and get on with the interview.

15) Do not dwell at length on your present job

The opening question may relate to your present assignment. Answer the question but do not go into an extended discussion. You are being examined for a *new* job, not your present one. As a matter of fact, try to phrase ALL your answers in terms of the job for which you are being examined.

Basis of Rating

Probably you will forget most of these "do's" and "don'ts" when you walk into the oral interview room. Even remembering them all will not ensure you a passing grade. Perhaps you did not have the qualifications in the first place. But remembering them will help you to put your best foot forward, without treading on the toes of the board members.

Rumor and popular opinion to the contrary notwithstanding, an oral board wants you to make the best appearance possible. They know you are under pressure – but they also want to see how you respond to it as a guide to what your reaction would be under the pressures of the job you seek. They will be influenced by the degree of poise you display, the personal traits you show and the manner in which you respond.

ABOUT THIS BOOK

This book contains tests divided into Examination Sections. Go through each test, answering every question in the margin. At the end of each test look at the answer key and check your answers. On the ones you got wrong, look at the right answer choice and learn. Do not fill in the answers first. Do not memorize the questions and answers, but understand the answer and principles involved. On your test, the questions will likely be different from the samples. Questions are changed and new ones added. If you understand these past questions you should have success with any changes that arise. Tests may consist of several types of questions. We have additional books on each subject should more study be advisable or necessary for you. Finally, the more you study, the better prepared you will be. This book is intended to be the last thing you study before you walk into the examination room. Prior study of relevant texts is also recommended. NLC publishes some of these in our Fundamental Series. Knowledge and good sense are important factors in passing your exam. Good luck also helps. So now study this Passbook, absorb the material contained within and take that knowledge into the examination. Then do your best to pass that exam.

EXAMINATION SECTION

ARITHMETICAL REASONING
EXAMINATION SECTION
TEST 1

DIRECTIONS: Each question or incomplete statement is followed by several suggested answers or completions. Select the one that BEST answers the question or completes the statement. *PRINT THE LETTER OF THE CORRECT ANSWER IN THE SPACE AT THE RIGHT.*

1. _____

1.

3" pipeline

←X→   8'3 1/2"   ←X→

8'9 3/4"

In the above sketch of a 3" pipeline, the distance X is MOST NEARLY _____ inches.

  A. 3 1/8   B. 3 1/2   C. 3 1/2   D. 3 5/8

2. The fraction 9/64 is MOST NEARLY equal to

  A. .1375   B. .1406   C. .1462   D. .1489

2. _____

3. The sum of the following dimensions 1'2 3/16",1'5 1/2", and 1'4 5/8" is

  A. 3'11 15/16"   B. 4' 5/16"
  C. 4'11/16"   D. 4'1 5/8"

3. _____

4. The scale on a plumbing drawing is 1/8" = 1 foot.
A horizontal line measuring 3 5/16" on the drawing would represent a length of _____ feet.

  A. 24.9   B. 26.5   C. 28.3   D. 30.2

4. _____

5. Assume that a water meter reads 50,631 cubic feet and the previous reading was 39,842 cubic feet.
If the charge for water is 23¢ per 100 cubic feet or any fraction thereof, the bill for the amount of water used since the previous meter reading will be

  A. $24.22   B. $24.38   C. $24.84   D. $24.95

5. _____

6. At a certain premises, the water consumption was 4 percent higher in 2015 than it was in 2014.
If the water consumption for 2015 was 9,740 cubic feet, then the water consumption for 2014 was MOST NEARLY _____ cubic feet.

  A. 9,320   B. 9,350   C. 9,365   D. 9,390

6. _____

7. A pump delivers water at a constant rate of 40 gallons per minute.
   If there are 7.5 gallons to a cubic foot of water, the time it will take to fill a tank 6 feet x 5 feet x 4 feet is MOST NEARLY _____ minutes.

   7._____

   A. 15   B. 22.5   C. 28.5   D. 30

8. The total weight, in pounds, of three lengths of 3" cast-iron pipe 7'6" long, weighing 14.5 pounds per foot, and four lengths of 4" cast-iron pipe each 5'0" long, weighing 13.0 pounds per foot, is MOST NEARLY

   8._____

   A. 540   B. 585   C. 600   D. 665

9. The water pressure at the bottom of a column of water 34 feet high is 14.7 lbs./sq.in. The water pressure in lbs./sq.in. at the bottom of the column of water 12 feet high is MOST NEARLY

   9._____

   A. 3   B. 5   C. 7   D. 9

10. The number of cubic yards of earth that would be removed when digging a trench 8 feet wide x 9 feet deep x 63 feet long is

    10._____

    A. 56   B. 168   C. 314   D. 504

11. On test, a meter registered one cubic foot for each 1 1/3 cubic feet of water that passed through it.
    If the meter had a reading of 1,200 cubic feet, we may conclude that the CORRECT amount should be _____ cubic feet.

    11._____

    A. 800   B. 900   C. 1,500   D. 1,600

12. A water use meter reads 87,463 cubic feet.
    If the previous reading was 17,377 cubic feet and the rate charged is 15 cents per 100 cubic feet, the bill for water use during this period is about

    12._____

    A. $45.00   B. $65.00   C. $85.00   D. $105.00

13. Under proper conditions, the one of the following groups of pipes that gives the same flow in gals/min as one 6" diameter pipe is (neglect friction) _____ pipes of _____ diameter each.

    13._____

    A. 3; 3"   B. 4; 3"   C. 2; 4"   D. 3; 4"

14. A roof tank is used to furnish the domestic water supply to a ten story building. This tank has a capacity of 5,900 gallons. At 10:00 A.M. one morning, the tank is half full.
    If water is being used at the rate of 50 gals/min, the pump which is used to fill the tank has a rated capacity of 90 gals/min, the time it would take to fill the tank under these conditions is MOST NEARLY _____ hour(s), _____ minutes.

    14._____

    A. 2; 8   B. 1; 14   C. 2; 32   D. 1; 2

15. The number of gallons of water contained in a cylindrical swimming pool 8 feet in diameter and filled to a depth of 3 feet 6 inches is MOST NEARLY (assume 7.5 gallons = 1 cubic foot)

    15._____

    A. 30   B. 225   C. 1,320   D. 3,000

16. The charge for metered water is 52 1/2 cents per hundred cubic feet, with a minimum charge of $21 per annum. Of the following, the SMALLEST water usage in hundred cubic feet that would result in a charge GREATER than the minimum is

    A. 39   B. 40   C. 41   D. 42

16._____

17. The annual frontage rent on a one-story building 40 ft. in length is $735.00. For each additional story, $52.50 per annum is added to the frontage rent. For demolition, the charge for wetting down is 3/8 of the annual frontage charge.
The charge for wetting down a building six stories in height, with a 40 ft. frontage, is MOST NEARLY

    A. $369   B. $371   C. $372   D. $374

17._____

18. If the drawing of a piping layout is made to a scale of 1/4" equals one foot, then a 7'9" length of piping would be represented by a scaled length on the drawing of APPROXI-MATELY _____ inches.

    A. 2   B. 7 3/4   C. 23 1/4   D. 31

18._____

19. A plumbing sketch is drawn to a scale of eighth-size. A line measuring 3" on the sketch would be equivalent to _____ feet.

    A. 2   B. 6   C. 12   D. 24

19._____

20. If 500 feet of pipe weighs 800 lbs., the number of pounds that 120 feet will weigh is MOST NEARLY

    A. 190   B. 210   C. 230   D. 240

20._____

21. If a trench is excavated 3'0" wide by 5'6" deep and 50 feet long, the total number of cubic yards of earth removed is MOST NEARLY

    A. 30   B. 90   C. 150   D. 825

21._____

22. Assume that a plumber earns $86,500 per year.
If eighteen percent of his pay is deducted for taxes and social security, his net weekly pay will be APPROXIMATELY

    A. $1,326   B. $1,365   C. $1,436   D. $1,457.50

22._____

23. Assume that a plumbing installation is made up of the following fixtures and groups of fix-tures: 12 bathroom groups each containing one W.C., one lavatory, and one bathtub with shower; 12 bathroom groups each containing one W.C., one lavatory, one bathtub, and one shower stall; 24 combination kitchen fixtures; 4 floor drains; 6 slop sinks without flushing rim; and 2 shower stalls (or shower bath).
The total number of fixtures for the above plumbing installation is MOST NEARLY

    A. 60   B. 95   C. 120   D. 210

23._____

24. A triangular opening in a wall forms a 30-60 degree right triangle.
If the longest side measures 12'0", then the shortest side will measure

    A. 3'0"   B. 4'0"   C. 6'0"   D. 8'0"

24._____

25. You are directed to cut 4 pieces of pipe, one each of the following length: 2'6 1/4",   25.____
3'9 3/8", 4'7 5/8", and 5'8 7/8".
The total length of these 4 pieces is

     A. 15'7 1/4"   B. 15'9 3/8"   C. 16'5 7/8"   D. 16'8 1/8"

KEY (CORRECT ANSWERS)

1.	A		11.	D
2.	B		12.	D
3.	B		13.	B
4.	B		14.	B
5.	C		15.	C
6.	C		16.	C
7.	B		17.	D
8.	B		18.	A
9.	B		19.	A
10.	B		20.	A

21.	A
22.	B
23.	C
24.	C
25.	D

SOLUTIONS TO PROBLEMS

1. 8'3 1/2" + x + x = 8'9 3/4" Then, 2x = 6 1/4", so x = 3 1/8"

2. 9/64 = .140625 = .1406

3. 1'2 3/16" + 1'5 1/2" +1'4 5/8" = 3'11 21/16" = 4'5/16"

4. 3 5/16" ÷ 1/8" =53/16 x 8/1 = 26.5. Then, (26.5)(1 ft.) = 26.5 feet

5. 50,631 - 39,842 = 10,789; 10,789 ÷ 100 = 107.89
   Since the cost is .23 per 100 cubic feet or any fraction thereof, the cost will be
   (.23)(107) + .23 = $24.84

6. 9740 ÷ 1.04 = 9365 cu.ft.

7. 40 ÷ 7.5 = 5 1/3 cu.ft. of water per minute. The volume = (6)(5)(4) = 120 cu.ft. Thus, the
   number of minutes needed to fill the tank is 120 ÷ 5 1/3 = 22.5

8. 3" pipe: 3 x 7'6" = 22 1/2' x 14.5 lbs. = 326.25
   4" pipe: 4 x 5' = 20' x 13 lbs. = 260
   326.25 + 260 = 586.25 (most nearly 585)

9. Let x = pressure. Then, 34/12 = 14.7/x. So, 34x = 176.4
   Solving, x ≈ 5 lbs./sq.in.

10. (8)(9)(63) = 4536 cu.ft. Since 1 cu.yd. = 27 cu.ft., 4536 cu.ft. is equivalent to 168 cu.yds.

11. Let x = correct amount. Then, $\frac{1}{1200}=\frac{1\frac{1}{3}}{x}$. Solving, x = 1600

12. 87,463 - 17,377 = 70,086; and 70,086 ÷ 100 = 700.86 ≈ 700 Then, (700)(.15) = $105.00

13. Cross-sectional area of a 6" diameter pipe = $(\pi)(3")^2 = 9\pi$ sq. in. Note that the combined cross-sectional areas of four 3" diameter pipes = $(4)(\pi)(1.5")^2 = 9\pi$ sq. in.

14. 90 - 50 = 40 gals/min. Then, 2950 ÷ 40 = 73.75 min. ≈ 1 hr. 14 min.

15. Volume = $(\pi)(4)^2(3 1/2) = 56\pi$ cu.ft. Then, $(56\pi)(7.5) = 1320$ gals.

16. For 4100 cu.ft., the charge of (.525)(41) = $21,525 > $21

17. Rent = $73,500 + (5)($52.50) = $997,50. For demolition, the charge = (3/8)($997.50)
    $374

18. (1/4")(7.75) = 2"

19. (3")(8) = 24" = 2 ft.

20. Let x = weight. Then, 500/800 = 120/x . Solving, x = 192 190 lbs.

21. (3')(5 1/2')(50') = 825 cu.ft. Then, 825 ÷ 27 ≈ 30 cu.yds.

22. Net pay = (.82)($86,500) = $70,930/yr. Weekly pay = $70,930 ÷ 52 ≈ $1365

23. (12x3) + (12x4) +24+4+6+2= 120

24. The shortest side = (1/2)(hypotenuse) = (1/2)(12') = 6'

25. 2'6 1/4" + 3'9 3/8" + 4'7 5/8" + 5'8 7/8 " = 14'30 17/8" = 16'8 1/8"

———————

TEST 2

DIRECTIONS: Each question or incomplete statement is followed by several suggested answers or completions. Select the one that BEST answers the question or completes the statement. *PRINT THE LETTER OF THE CORRECT ANSWER IN THE SPACE AT THE RIGHT.*

1. The sum of the following pipe lengths, 15 5/8", 8 3/4", 30 5/16" and 20 1/2", is   1._____

   A. 77 1/8"   B. 76 3/16"   C. 75 3/16"   D. 74 5/16"

2. If the outside diameter of a pipe is 6 inches and the wall thickness is 1/2 inch, the inside   2._____
   area of this pipe, in square inches, is MOST NEARLY

   A. 15.7   B. 17.3   C. 19.6   D. 23.8

3. Three lengths of pipe 1'10", 3'2 1/2", and 5'7 1/2", respectively, are to be cut from a pipe   3._____
   14'0" long.
   Allowing 1/8" for each pipe cut, the length of pipe remaining is

   A. 3'1 1/8"   B. 3'2 1/2"   C. 3'3 1/4"   D. 3'3 5/8"

4. According to the building code, the MAXIMUM permitted surface temperature of combus-   4._____
   tible construction materials located near heating equipment is 76.5°C. ($°F=(°Cx9/5)+32$)
   Maximum temperature Fahrenheit is MOST NEARLY

   A. 170° F   B. 195° F   C. 210° F   D. 220° F

5. A pump discharges 7.5 gals/minutes.   5._____
   In 2.5 hours the pump will discharge _____ gallons.

   A. 1125   B. 1875   C. 1950   D. 2200

6. A pipe with an outside diameter of 4" has a circumference of MOST NEARLY _____   6._____
   inches.

   A. 8.05   B. 9.81   C. 12.57   D. 14.92

7. A piping sketch is drawn to a scale of 1/8" = 1 foot.   7._____
   A vertical steam line measuring 3 1/2" on the sketch would have an ACTUAL length of
   _____ feet.

   A. 16   B. 22   C. 24   D. 28

8. A pipe having an inside diameter of 3.48 inches and a wall thickness of .18 inches will   8._____
   have an outside diameter of _____ inches.

   A. 3.84   B. 3.64   C. 3.57   D. 3.51

9. A rectangular steel bar having a volume of 30 cubic inches, a width of 2 inches, and a   9._____
   height of 3 inches will have a length of _____ inches.

   A. 12   B. 10   C. 8   D. 5

10. A pipe weighs 20.4 pounds per foot of length.   10._____
    The total weight of eight pieces of this pipe with each piece 20 feet in length is MOST
    NEARLY _____ pounds.

    A. 460   B. 1,680   C. 2,420   D. 3,260

11. Assume that four pieces of pipe measuring 2'1 1/4", 4'2 3/4", 5'1 9/16", and 6'3 5/8",   11.____
respectively, are cut with a saw from a pipe 20"0" long.
Allowing 1/16" waste for each cut, the length of the remaining pipe is

    A. 2'1 9/16"   B. 2'2 9/16"   C. 2'4 13/16"   D. 2'8 9/16"

12. If one cubic inch of steel weighs 0.28 pounds, the weight, in pounds, of a steel bar 1/2" x   12.____
6" x 2'0" long is MOST NEARLY

    A. 11   B. 16   C. 20   D. 24

13. If the circumference of a circle is equal to 31.416 inches, then its diameter, in inches, is   13.____
equal to MOST NEARLY

    A. 8   B. 9   C. 10   D. 13

14. Assume that a steam fitter's helper receives a salary of $171.36 a day for 250 days is   14.____
considered a full work year. If taxes, social security, hospitalization, and pension
deducted from his salary amounts to 16 percent of his gross pay, then his net yearly salary will be MOST NEARLY

    A. $31,788   B. $35,982   C. $41,982   D. $42,840

15. If the outside diameter of a pipe is 14 inches and the wall thickness is 1/2 inch, then the   15.____
inside area of the pipe, in square inches, is MOST NEARLY

    A. 125   B. 133   C. 143   D. 154

16. A steam leak in a pipe line allows steam to escape at a rate of 50,000 pounds each   16.____
month.
Assuming that the cost of steam is $2.50 per 1,000 pounds, the TOTAL cost of wasted
steam from this leak for a 12-month period would amount to

    A. $125   B. $300   C. $1,500   D. $3,000

17. If 250 feet of 4" pipe weighs 400 pounds, the weight of this pipe per linear foot is _____   17.____
pounds.

    A. 1.25   B. 1.50   C. 1.60   D. 1.75

18. A set of heating plan drawings is drawn to a scale of 1/4" = 1 foot.   18.____
If a length of pipe measures 4 5/8" on the drawing, the ACTUAL length of the pipe, in
feet, is

    A. 16.3   B. 16.8   C. 17.5   D. 18.5

19. The TOTAL length of four pieces of pipe whose lengths are 3'4 1/2", 2'1 5/16", 4'9 3/8",   19.____
and 2'3 1/4", respectively, is

    A. 11'5 7/16"   B. 11'6 7/16"
    C. 12'5 7/16"   D. 12'6 7/16"

20. Assume that a pipe trench is 3 feet wide, 3 feet deep, and 300 feet long.   20.____
If the unit cost of excavating the trench is $120 per cubic yard, the TOTAL cost of exca-
vating the trench is

    A. $1,200   B. $12,000   C. $27,000   D. $36,000

21. The TOTAL length of four pieces of 1 1/2" galvanized steel pipe whose lengths are 7 ft. + 3 1/2 inches, 4 ft. + 2 1/4 inches, 6 ft. + 7 inches, and 8 ft. +5 1/8 inches is

21.____

    A. 26 feet + 5 7/8 inches   B. 25 ft. + 6 7/8 inches
    C. 25 feet + 4 1/4 inches   D. 25 ft. + 3 3/8 inches

22. A swimming pool is 25' wide by 75' long and has an average depth of 5'. 1 cubic foot contains 7.5 gallons of water. The capacity, when filled to the overflow, is _____ gallons.

22.____

    A. 9,375   B. 65,625   C. 69,005   D. 70,312

23. The sum of 3 1/4, 5 1/8, 2 1/2 , and 3 3/8 is

23.____

    A. 14   B. 14 1/8   C. 14 1/4   D. 14 3/8

24. Assume that it takes 6 men 8 days to do a particular job. If you have only 4 men available to do this job and they all work at the same speed, then the number of days it would take to complete the job would be

24.____

    A. 11   B. 12   C. 13   D. 14

25. The total length of four pieces of 2" O.D. pipe, whose lengths are 7'3 1/2", 4'2 3/16", 5'7 5/16", and 8'5 7/8", respectively, is MOST NEARLY

25.____

    A. 24'6 3/4"   B. 24'7 15/16"
    C. 25'5 13/16"   D. 25'6 7/8"

KEY (CORRECT ANSWERS)

1.	C	11.	B
2.	C	12.	C
3.	D	13.	C
4.	A	14.	B
5.	A	15.	B
6.	C	16.	C
7.	D	17.	C
8.	A	18.	D
9.	D	19.	D
10.	D	20.	B

21.	A
22.	D
23.	C
24.	B
25.	D

SOLUTIONS TO PROBLEMS

1. 15 5/8" + 8 3/4" + 30 5/16" + 20 1/2" = 73 35/16" = 75 3/16"

2. Inside diameter = 6" - 1/2" - 1/2" = 5". Area = (π)(5/2")^2 ≈ 19.6 sq. in.

3. Pipe remaining = 14' - 1'10" - 3'2 1/2" - 5'7 1/2" - (3)(1/8") = 3'3 5/8"

4. 76.5 x 9/5 = 137.7 + 32 = 169.7

5. 7.5 x 150 = 1125

6. Radius = 2" Circumference = (2π)(2") ≈ 12.57"

7. 3 1/2" 1/8" = (7/2)(8/1) = 28 Then, (28)(1 ft.) = 28 feet

8. Outside diameter = 3.48" + .18" + .18" = 3.84"

9. 30 = (2)(3)(length). So, length = 5"

10. Total weight = (20.4)(8)(20) ≈ 3260 lbs.

11. 20' - 2'1 1/4" - 4'2 3/4" - 5'1 9/16" - 6'3 5/8" - (4)(1/16") = 2'2 9/16"

12. Weight = (.28)(1/2")(6")(24") = 20.16 ≈ 20 lbs.

13. Diameter = 31.416" ÷ π ≈ 10"

14. His net pay for 250 days = (.84)($171.36)(250) = $35,985.60 ≈ $35,928 (from answer key)

15. Inside diameter = 14" - 1/2" - 1/2" = 13". Area = (π)(13/2")^2 ≈ 133 sq.in

16. (50,000 lbs.)(12) = 600,000 lbs. per year. The cost would be ($2.50)(600) = $1500

17. 400 ÷ 250 = 1.60 pounds per linear foot

18. 4 5/8" ÷ 1/4" = 37/8 . 4/1 = 18.5 Then, (18.5)(1 ft.) = 18.5 feet

19. 3'4 1/2" + 2'1 5/16" + 4'9 3/8" + 2'3 1/4" = 11'17 23/16" = 12'6 7/16"

20. (3')(3')(300') = 2700 cu.ft., which is 2700 ÷ 27 = 100 cu.yds. Total cost = ($120)(100) = $12,000

21. 7'3 1/2" + 4'2 1/4" + 6'7" + 8'5 1/8" = 25'17 7/8" = 26'5 7/8"

22. (25)(75)(5) = 9375 cu.ft. Then, (9375)(7.5) ≈ 70,312 gals.

23. 3 1/4 + 5 1/8 + 2 1/2 + 3 3/8 = 13 10/8 = 14 1/4

24. (6) (8) = 48 man-days. Then, 48 ÷ 4 = 12 days

25. 7'3 1/2" + 4'2 3/16" + 5'7 5/16" + 8'5 7/8" = 24'17 30/16" = 25'6 7/8"

───────

TEST 3

DIRECTIONS: Each question or incomplete statement is followed by several suggested answers or completions. Select the one that BEST answers the question or completes the statement. *PRINT THE LETTER OF THE CORRECT ANSWER IN THE SPACE AT THE RIGHT.*

1. The time required to pump 2,500 gallons of water out of a sump at the rate of 12 1/2 gallons per minutes would be _____ hour(s) _____ minutes.

   A. 1; 40   B. 2; 30   C. 3; 20   D. 6; 40

   1.____

2. Copper tubing which has an inside diameter of 1 1/16" and a wall thickness of .095" has an outside diameter which is MOST NEARLY _____ inches.

   A. 1 5/32   B. 1 3/16   C. 1 7/32   D. 1 1/4

   2.____

3. Assume that 90 gallons per minute flow through a certain 3-inch pipe which is tapped into a street main.
   The amount of water which would flow through a 1-inch pipe tapped into the same street main is MOST NEARLY _____ gpm.

   A. 90   B. 45   C. 30   D. 10

   3.____

4. The weight of a 6 foot length of 8-inch pipe which weighs 24.70 pounds per foot is _____ lbs.

   A. 148.2   B. 176.8   C. 197.6   D. 212.4

   4.____

5. If a 4-inch pipe is directly coupled to a 2-inch pipe and 16 gallons per minute are flowing through the 4-inch pipe, then the flow through the 2-inch pipe will be _____ gallons per minute.

   A. 4   B. 8   C. 16   D. 32

   5.____

6. If the water pressure at the bottom of a column of water 34 feet high is 14.7 pounds per square inch, the water pressure at the bottom of a column of water 18 feet high is MOST NEARLY _____ pounds per square inch.

   A. 8.0   B. 7.8   C. 7.6   D. 7.4

   6.____

7. If there are 7 1/2 gallons in a cubic foot of water and if water flows from a hose at a constant rate of 4 gallons per minute, the time it should take to COMPLETELY fill a tank of 1,600 cubic feet capacity with water from that hose is _____ hours.

   A. 300   B. 150   C. 100   D. 50

   7.____

8. Each of a group of fifteen water meter readers read an average of 62 water meters a day in a certain 5-day work week. A total of 5,115 meters are read by this group the following week.
   The TOTAL number of meters read in the second week as compared to the first week shows a

   A. 10% increase   B. 15% increase
   C. 20% increase   D. 5% decrease

   8.____

9. A certain water consumer used 5% more water in 1994 than he did in 1993.   9.____
If his water consumption for 1994 was 8,375 cubic feet, the amount of water he consumed in 1993 was MOST NEARLY _____ cubic feet.

     A. 9,014   B. 8,816   C. 7,976   D. 6,776

10. Assume that a water meter reads 40,175 cubic feet and that the previous reading was   10.____
29,186 cubic feet.
If the charge for water is 92 cents per 100 cubic feet or any fraction thereof, the bill for
the amount of water used since the previous meter reading should be

     A. $100.28   B. $101.04   C. $101.08   D. $101.20

11. A leaking faucet caused a loss of 216 cubic feet of water in a 30-day month.   11.____
If there are 7.5 gallons in a cubic foot of water, then the AVERAGE loss of water per
hour for that month was _____ gallons.

     A. 2 1/4   B. 2 1/8   C. 2   D. 1 3/4

12. The fraction which is equal to .375 is   12.____

     A. 3/16   B. 5/32   C. 3/8   D. 5/12

13. A square backyard swimming pool, each side of which is 10 feet long, is filled to a depth   13.____
of 3 1/2 feet.
If there are 7 1/2 gallons in a cubic foot of water, the number of gallons of water in the
pool is MOST NEARLY _____ gallons.

     A. 46.7   B. 100   C. 2,625   D. 3,500

14. When 1 5/8, 3 3/4, 6 1/3, and 9 1/2 are added, the resulting sum is   14.____

     A. 21 1/8   B. 21 1/6   C. 21 5/24   D. 21 1/4

15. When 946 1/2 is subtracted from 1,035 1/4, the result is   15.____

     A. 87 1/4   B. 87 3/4   C. 88 1/4   D. 88 3/4

16. When 39 is multiplied by 697, the result is   16.____

     A. 8,364   B. 26,283   C. 27,183   D. 28,003

17. When 16.074 is divided by .045, the result is   17.____

     A. 3.6   B. 35.7   C. 357.2   D. 3,572

18. To dig a trench 3'0" wide, 50'0" long, and 5'6" deep, the total number of cubic yards of   18.____
earth to be removed is MOST NEARLY

     A. 30   B. 90   C. 140   D. 825

19. The TOTAL length of four pieces of 2" pipe, whose lengths are 7'3 1/2", 4'2 3/16",   19.____
5'7 5/16", and 8'5 7/8", respectively, is

     A. 24'6 3/4"   B. 24'7 15/16"
     C. 25'5 13/16"   D. 25'6 7/8"

20. A hot water line made of copper has a straight horizontal run of 150 feet and, when   20.____
     installed, is at a temperature of 45° F. In use, its temperature rises to 190° F.
     If the coefficient of expansion for copper is 0.0000095" per foot per degree F, the
     TOTAL expansion, in inches, in the run of pipe is given by the product of 150 multiplied
     by 0.0000095 by

     A. 145   B. 145 x 12
     C. 145 divided by 12   D. 145 x 12 x 12

21. A water storage tank measures 5' long, 4' wide, and 6' deep and is filled to the 5 1/2'   21.____
     mark with water.
     If one cubic foot of water weighs 62 pounds, the number of pounds of water required to
     COMPLETELY fill the tank is

     A. 7,440   B. 6,200   C. 1,240   D. 620

22. Assume that a pipe worker earns $83,125.00 per year.   22.____
     If seventeen percent of his pay is deducted for taxes, social security, and pension, his
     net weekly pay will be APPROXIMATELY

     A. $1598.50   B. $1504.00   C. $1453.00   D. $1325.00

23. If eighteen feet of 4" cast iron pipe weighs approximately 390 pounds, the weight of this   23.____
     pipe per lineal foot will be MOST NEARLY _____ lbs.

     A. 19   B. 22   C. 23   D. 25

24. If it takes 3 men 11 days to dig a trench, the number of days it will take 5 men to dig the   24.____
     same trench, assuming all work is done at the same rate of speed, is MOST NEARLY

     A. 6 1/2   B. 7 3/4   C. 8 1/4   D. 8 3/4

25. If a trench is dug 6'0" deep, 2'6" wide, and 8'0" long, the area of the opening, in square   25.____
     feet, is MOST NEARLY

     A. 48   B. 32   C. 20   D. 15

KEY (CORRECT ANSWERS)

1.	C		11.	A
2.	D		12.	C
3.	D		13.	C
4.	A		14.	C
5.	B		15.	D
6.	B		16.	C
7.	D		17.	C
8.	A		18.	A
9.	C		19.	D
10.	D		20.	A

21.	D
22.	D
23.	B
24.	A
25.	C

SOLUTIONS TO PROBLEMS

1. 2500 ÷ 12 1/2 = 200 min. = 3 hrs. 20 min.

2. 1 1/16" + .095" + .095" = 1.0625 + .095 + .095 = 1.2525" ≈ 1 1/4"

3. Cross-sectional areas for a 3-inch pipe and a 1-inch pipe are $(\pi)(1.5)^2$ and $(\pi)(.5)^2 =$ 2.25 π and .25 π, respectively. Let x = amount of water flowing through the 1-inch pipe. Then, $\frac{90}{x} = \frac{2.25\pi}{.25\pi}$. Solving, x = 10 gals/min

4. (24.70)(6) = 148.2 lbs.

5. $\frac{4" \text{ pipe}}{16 \text{ gallons}} = \frac{2" \text{ pipe}}{x \text{ gallons}}$, 4x = 32, x = 8

6. Let x = pressure. Then, 34/18 = 14.7/x . Solving, x ≈ 7.8

7. (1600)(7.5) = 12,000 gallons. Then, 12,000 ÷ 4 = 3000 min. = 50 hours

8. (15)(62)(5) = 4650. Then, (5115-4650)/4650 = 10% increase

9. 8375 ÷ 1.05 ≈ 7976 cu.ft.

10. 40,175 - 29,186 = 10,989 cu.ft. Then, 10,989 100 = 109.89. Since .92 is charged for each 100 cu.ft. or fraction thereof, total cost = (.92)(110) = $101.20

11. (216)(7.5) = 1620 gallons. In 30 days, there are 720 hours. Thus, the average water loss per hour = 1620 ÷ 720 = 2 1/4 gallons.

12. .375 = 375/1000 = 3/8

13. Volume = (10)(10)(3 1/2) = 350 cu.ft. Then, (350)(7 1/2) = 2625 gallons

14. 1 5/8 + 3 3/4 + 6 1/3 + 9 1/2 = 19 53/24 = 21 5/24

15. 1035 1/4 - 946 1/2 = 88 3/4

16. (39)(697) = 27,183

17. 16.074 .045 = 357.2

18. (3')(50')(5 1/2') = 825 cu.ft. ≈ 30 cu.yds., since 1 cu.yd. = 27 cu.ft.

19. 7'3 1/2" + 4'2 3/16" + 5'7 5/16" + 8'5 7/8" = 24'17 30/16" = 25'6 7/8"

20. Total expansion = (150)(.0000095)(145)

21. Number of pounds needed = (5) (4)(6-5 1/2)(62) = 620

22. Net annual pay = ($83,125)(.83) $\approx$ $69000. Then, the net weekly pay = $69000 $\div$ 52 $\approx$ $1325 (actually about $1327)

23. 390 lbs. $\div$ 18 = 21.6 lbs. per linear foot

24. (3)(11) = 33 man-days. Then, 33 $\div$ 5 = 6.6 $\approx$ 6 1/2 days

25. Area = (8')(2 1/2') = 20 sq.ft.

———

ARITHMETICAL REASONING

EXAMINATION SECTION
TEST 1

DIRECTIONS: Each question or incomplete statement is followed by several suggested answers or completions. Select the one that BEST answers the question or completes the statement. *PRINT THE LETTER OF THE CORRECT ANSWER IN THE SPACE AT THE RIGHT.*

1. If it takes 2 men 9 days to do a job, how many men are needed to do the same job in 3 days?

    A. 4   B. 5   C. 6   D. 7

1.____

2. Suppose that a department operates 1,644 buildings. If one employee is needed for every 2 buildings, and one foreman is needed for every 18 employees, the number of foremen needed is CLOSEST to

    A. 45   B. 50   C. 55   D. 60

2.____

3. If 60 bars of soap cost the same as 2 gallons of wax, how many bars of soap can be bought for the price of 5 gallons of wax?

    A. 120   B. 150   C. 180   D. 300

3.____

4. An employee waxes 275 sq.ft. of floor on Monday, 352 sq.ft. on Tuesday, 179 sq.ft. on Wednesday, and 302 sq.ft. on Thursday.
In order to average 280 sq.ft. of floor waxed a day, how many square feet of floor must he wax on Friday?

    A. 264   B. 278   C. 292   D. 358

4.____

5. A project covers 35 acres altogether. Lawns, playgrounds, and walks take up 28 acres and the rest is given over to buildings.
What percentage of the total area is given over to buildings?

    A. 7%   B. 20%   C. 25%   D. 28%

5.____

6. When preparing for a mopping operation, fill the standard 16 quart bucket to the 3/4 full mark with warm water. Then add detergent at the rate of 2 oz. per gallon of water and disinfectant at the rate of 1 oz. to 3 gallons of water. According to these directions, the amount of detergent and disinfectant to add to 3/4 of a bucket of warm water is _____ oz. detergent and _____ oz. disinfectant.

    A. 4; 1/2   B. 5; 3/4   C. 6; 1   D. 8; 1 1/4

6.____

7. If corn brooms weigh 32 lbs. a dozen, the average weight of one corn broom is CLOSEST to _____ lbs. _____ oz.

    A. 2; 14   B. 2; 11   C. 2; 9   D. 2; 6

7.____

8. At the beginning of the year, a foreman has 7 dozen electric bulbs in stock. During the year, he receives a shipment of 14 dozen bulbs, and also replaces 5 burned out bulbs a month in each of 3 buildings in his area. How many electric bulbs does he have on hand at the end of the year? _____ dozen.

    A. 3   B. 6   C. 8   D. 12

8.____

9. A project has 4 buildings, each 14 floors high. Each floor has 10 apartments. If 35% of the apartments in the project have 3 rooms or less, how many apartments have 4 or more rooms?

    A. 196   B. 210   C. 364   D. 406

9.____

10. An employee takes 1 hour and 30 minutes a day to sweep 30 flights of stairs. How many flights of stairs does he sweep in a month if he spends a total of 30 hours doing this job and works at the same rate?

    A. 200   B. 300   C. 600   D. 900

10.____

11. During a month, Employee A washed 30 windows, Employee B washed 4 times as many windows as Employee A, and Employee C washed half as many windows as Employee B. The TOTAL number of windows washed by all three men together during this month is

    A. 180   B. 210   C. 240   D. 330

11.____

12. How much would it cost to completely fence in the playground area shown at the right with fencing costing $7.50 a foot?
    A. $615.00
    B. $820.00
    C. $885.00
    D. $960.00

12.____

14 FT.

9 FT.

26 FT.

33 FT.

13. A drill bit measures .625 inches. The fractional equivalent, in inches, is

    A. 9/16   B. 5/8   C. 11/16   D. 3/4

13.____

14. The number of cubic yards of sand required to fill a bin measuring 12 feet by 6 feet by 4 feet is MOST NEARLY

    A. 8   B. 11   C. 48   D. 96

14.____

15. Assume that you are assigned to put down floor tiles in a room measuring 8 feet by 10 feet. Individual tiles measure 9 inches by 9 inches.
The total number of floor tiles required to cover the entire floor is MOST NEARLY

    A. 107   B. 121   C. 142   D. 160

15.____

16. Lumber is usually sold by the board foot, and a board foot is defined as a board one foot square and one inch thick.
If the price of one board foot of lumber is 90 cents and you need 20 feet of lumber 6 inches wide and 1 inch thick, the cost of the 20 feet of lumber is

    A. $9.00   B. $12.00   C. $18.00   D. $24.00

16.____

17. For a certain plumbing repair job, you need three lengths of pipe, 12 1/4 inches, 6 1/2 inches, and 8 5/8 inches.
If you cut these three lengths from the same piece of pipe, which is 36 inches long, and each cut consumes 1/8 inch of pipe, the length of pipe REMAINING after you have cut out your three pieces should be _____ inches.

    A. 7 1/4   B. 7 7/8   C. 8 1/4   D. 8 7/8

17.____

18. A maintenance bond for a roadway pavement is in an amount of 10% of the estimated cost.
If the estimated cost is $8,000,000, the maintenance bond is

    A. $8,000   B. $80,000   C. $800,000   D. $8,000,000

18.____

19. Specifications require that a core be taken every 700 square yards of paved roadway or fraction thereof. A 100 foot by 200 foot rectangular area would require _____ core(s).

    A. 1   B. 2   C. 3   D. 4

19.____

20. An applicant must file a map at a scale of 1" = 40'. Six inches on the map represents _____ feet on the ground.

    A. 600   B. 240   C. 120   D. 60

20.____

21. A 100' x 110' lot has an area of MOST NEARLY _____ acre.

    A. 1/8   B. 1/4   C. 3/8   D. 1/2

21.____

22. 1 inch is MOST NEARLY equal to _____ feet.

    A. .02   B. .04   C. .06   D. .08

22.____

23. The area of the triangle EFG shown at the right is MOST NEARLY _____ sq. ft.

    A. 36   B. 42   C. 48   D. 54

(Triangle EFG with apex F, base from E to G. Base segments labeled 8' and 4', with vertical heights 6' and 4'.)

23.____

24. Specifications state: As further security for the faithful performance of this contract, the Comptroller shall deduct, and retain until the final payment, 10% of the value of the work certified for payment in each partial payment voucher, until the amount so deducted and retained shall equal 5% of the contract price or in the case of a unit price contract, 5% of the estimated amount to be paid to the Contractor under the contract.
For a $300,000 contract, the amount to be retained at the end of the contract is

    A. $5,000   B. $10,000   C. $15,000   D. $20,000

24.____

25. Asphalt was laid for a length of 210 feet on the entire width of a street whose curb-to-curb distance is 30 feet. The number of square yards covered with asphalt is MOST NEARLY

    A. 210   B. 700   C. 2,100   D. 6,300

25.____

KEY (CORRECT ANSWERS)

1.	C		11.	B
2.	A		12.	C
3.	B		13.	B
4.	C		14.	B
5.	B		15.	C
6.	C		16.	A
7.	B		17.	C
8.	B		18.	C
9.	C		19.	D
10.	C		20.	B

21.	B
22.	D
23.	A
24.	C
25.	B

SOLUTIONS TO PROBLEMS

1. (2)(9) = 18 man-days. Then, 18 ÷ 3 = 6 men

2. The number of employees = 1644 ÷ 2 = 822. The number of foremen needed
    = 822 ÷ 18 ≈ 45

3. 1 gallon of wax costs the same as 60 ÷ 2 = 30 bars of soap. Thus, 5 gallons of wax costs
    the same as (5)(30) = 150 bars of soap.

4. To average 280 sq.ft. for five days means a total of (5)(280) = 1400 sq.ft. for all five days.
    The number of square feet to be waxed on Friday = 1400 - (275+352+179+302) = 292

5. The acreage for buildings is 35 - 28 = 7. Then, 7/35 = 20%

6. (16)(3/4) = 12 quarts = 3 gallons. The amount of detergent, in ounces, is (2)(3) = 6. The
    amount of disinfectant is 1 oz.

7. One corn broom weighs 32 ÷ 12 = 2 2/3 lbs. ≈ 2 lbs. 11 oz.

8. Number of bulbs at the beginning of the year = (7)(12) + (14)(12) = 252. Number of bulbs
    replaced over an entire year = (5)(3)(12) = 180. The number of unused bulbs = 252 - 180
    = 72 = 6 dozen.

9. Total number of apartments = (4)(14)(10) = 560. The number of apartments with at least
    4 rooms = (.65)(560) = 364.

10. 30 ÷ 1 1/2 = 20. Then, (20)(30) = 600 flights of stairs

11. The number of windows washed by A, B, C were 30, 120, and 60. Their total is 210.

12. The two missing dimensions are 26 - 14 = 12 ft. and 33 - 9 = 24 ft. Perimeter = 9 + 12 +
     33 + 26 + 24 + 14 = 118 ft. Thus, total cost of fencing = (118)($7.50) = $885.00

13. $.625 = \dfrac{625}{1000} = \dfrac{5}{8}$

14. (12)(6)(4) = 288 cu.ft. Now, 1 cu.yd. = 27 cu.ft.; 288 cu.ft. is equivalent to 10 2/3 or about
     11 cu.yds.

15. 144 sq.in. = 1 sq.ft. The room measures (8 ft.)x(10 ft.) = 80 sq.ft. = 11,520 sq.in. Each tile
     measures (9)(9) = 81 sq.in. The number of tiles needed = 11,520 ÷ 81 = 142.2 or about
     142.

16. 20 ft. by 6 in. = (20 ft.)(1/2 ft.) = 10 sq.ft. Then, (10X.90) = $9.00

17. There will be 3 cuts in making 3 lengths of pipe, and these 3 cuts will use (3)(1/8) = 3/8
     in. of pipe. The amount of pipe remaining after the 3 pieces are removed = 36 - 12 1/4
     - 6 1/2 - 8 5/8 - 3/8 = 8 1/4 in.

18. The maintenance bond = (.10)($8,000,000) = $800,000

19. (100)(200) = 20,000 sq.ft. = 20,000 ÷ 9 ≈ 2222 sq.yds. Then, 2222 ÷ 700 ≈ 3.17. Since a core must be taken for each 700 sq.yds. plus any left over fraction, 4 cores will be needed.

20. Six inches means (6)(40) = 240 ft. of actual length.

21. (100 ft.)(110 ft.) = 11,000 sq.ft. ≈ 1222 sq.yds. Then, since 1 acre = 4840 sq.yds., 1222 sq.yds. is equivalent to about 1/4 acre.

22. 1 in. = 1/12 ft. ≈ .08 ft.

23. Area of $\triangle$ EFG = (1/2)(8)(6) + (1/2)(4)(6) = 36 sq.ft.

24. The amount to be retained = (.05)($300,000) = $15,000

25. (210)(30) = 6300 sq.ft. Since 1 sq.yd. = 9 sq.ft., 6300 sq.ft. equals 700 sq.yds.

——————

TEST 2

DIRECTIONS: Each question or incomplete statement is followed by several suggested answers or completions. Select the one that BEST answers the question or completes the statement. *PRINT THE LETTER OF THE CORRECT ANSWER IN THE SPACE AT THE RIGHT.*

1. The TOTAL length of four pieces of 2" pipe, whose lengths are 7'3 1/2", 4'2 3/16", 5'7 5/16", and 8'5 7/8", respectively, is

   A.   24'6 3/4"   B.   24'7 15/16"
   C.   25'5 13/16"   D.   25'6 7/8"

1.____

2. Under the same conditions, the group of pipes that gives the SAME flow as one 6" pipe is (neglecting friction) _____ pipes.

   A. 3 3"   B. 4 3"   C. 2 4"   D. 3 4"

2.____

3. A water storage tank measures 5' long, 4' wide, and 6' deep and is filled to the 5 1/2' mark with water.
   If one cubic foot of water weighs 62 pounds, the number of pounds of water required to COMPLETELY fill the tank is

   A. 7,440   B. 6,200   C. 1,240   D. 620

3.____

4. A hot water line made of copper has a straight horizontal run of 150 feet and, when installed, is at a temperature of 45°F. In use, its temperature rises to 190°F.
   If the coefficient of expansion for copper is 0.0000095" per foot per degree F, the total expansion, in inches, in the run of pipe is given by the product of 150 multiplied by 0.0000095 by

   A.   145   B.   145 x 12
   C.   145 divided by 12   D.   145 x 12 x 12

4.____

5. To dig a trench 3'0" wide, 50'0" long, and 5'6" deep, the total number of cubic yards of earth to be removed is MOST NEARLY

   A. 30   B. 90   C. 140   D. 825

5.____

6. If it costs $65 for 20 feet of subway rail, the cost of 150 feet of this rail will be

   A. $487.50   B. $512.00   C. $589.50   D. $650.00

6.____

7. The number of cubic feet of concrete it takes to fill a form 10 feet long, 3 feet wide, and 6 inches deep is

   A. 12   B. 15   C. 20   D. 180

7.____

8. The sum of 4 1/16, 51/4, 3 5/8, and 4 7/16 is

   A. 17 3/16   B. 17 1/4   C. 17 5/16   D. 17 3/8

8.____

9. If you earn $10.20 per hour and time and one-half for working over 40 hours, your gross salary for a week in which you worked 42 hours would be

   A. $408.00   B. $428.40   C. $438.60   D. $770.80

9.____

10. A drill bit, used to drill holes in track ties, has a diameter of 0.75 inches. 10._____
When expressed as a fraction, the diameter of this drill bit is

    A. 1/4"   B. 3/8"   C. 1/2"   D. 3/4"

11. Three dozen shovels were purchased for use. 11._____
If the shovels were used at the rate of nine a week, the number of weeks that the three dozen lasted was

    A. 3   B. 4   C. 9   D. 12

12. Assume that you earn $20,000 per year. 12._____
If twenty percent of your pay is deducted for taxes, social security, and pension, your weekly take-home pay will be MOST NEARLY

    A. $280   B. $308   C. $328   D. $344

13. If a measurement scaled from a drawing is one inch, and the scale of the drawing is 1/8 13._____
inch to the foot, then the one inch measurement would represent an ACTUAL length of

    A. 8 feet   B. 2 feet
    C. 1/8 of a foot   D. 8 inches

14. Tiles 12" x 12" are used to lay a floor having the dimensions 10'0" x 12'0". 14._____
The MINIMUM number of tiles needed to completely cover the floor is

    A. 60   B. 96   C. 120   D. 144

15. The volume of concrete in a strip of sidewalk 30 feet long by 4 feet wide by 3 inches thick 15._____
is _____ cubic feet.

    A. 30   B. 120   C. 240   D. 360

16. To change a quantity of cubic feet into an equivalent quantity of cubic yards, _____ the 16._____
quantity by _____.

    A. multiply; 9   B. divide; 9
    C. multiply; 27   D. divide; 27

17. If a pump can deliver 50 gallons of water per minute, then the time needed for this pump 17._____
to empty an excavation containing 5,800 gallons of water is _____ hour(s) _____ minutes.

    A. 2; 12   B. 1; 56   C. 1; 44   D. 1; 32

18. The sum of 3 1/6", 4 1/4", 3 5/8", and 5 7/16" is 18._____

    A. 15 9/16"   B. 16 1/8"   C. 16 23/48"   D. 16 3/4"

19. If a measurement scaled from a drawing is 2 inches, and the scale of the drawing is 1/8 19._____
inch to the foot, then the two inch measurement would represent an ACTUAL length of

    A. 8 feet   B. 4 feet
    C. 1/4 of a foot   D. 16 feet

20. A room is 7'6" wide by 9'0" long with a ceiling height of 8'0". One gallon of flat paint will cover approximately 400 square feet of wall.
The number of gallons of this paint required to paint the walls of this room, making no deductions for windows or doors, is MOST NEARLY

    A. 1/4   B. 1/2   C. 2/3   D. 1

20.____

21. The cost of a certain job is broken down as follows:

        Materials $3,750
        Rental of equipment   1,200
        Labor   3,150

The percentage of the total cost of the job that can be charged to materials is MOST NEARLY

    A. 40%   B. 42%   C. 44%   D. 46%

21.____

22. By trial, it is found that by using two cubic feet of sand, a 5 cubic foot batch of concrete is produced. Using the same proportions, the amount of sand required
to produce 2 cubic yards of concrete is MOST NEARLY _____ cubic feet.

    A. 20   B. 22   C. 24   D. 26

22.____

23. It takes 4 men 6 days to do a certain job.
Working at the same speed, the number of days it will take 3 men to do this job is

    A. 7   B. 8   C. 9   D. 10

23.____

24. The cost of rawl plugs is $27.50 per gross. The cost of 2,448 rawl plugs is

    A. $467.50   B. $472.50   C. $477.50   D. $482.50

24.____

25. In a certain district, the area of a building may be no longer than 55% of the area of the lot on which it stands. On a rectangular lot 75 ft. by 125 ft., the maximum permissible area of building is, in square feet, MOST NEARLY

    A. 5,148   B. 5,152   C. 5,156   D. 5,160

25.____

KEY (CORRECT ANSWERS)

1.	D		11.	B
2.	B		12.	B
3.	D		13.	A
4.	A		14.	C
5.	A		15.	A
6.	A		16.	D
7.	B		17.	B
8.	D		18.	C
9.	C		19.	D
10.	D		20.	C

21.	D
22.	B
23.	B
24.	A
25.	C

———

SOLUTIONS TO PROBLEMS

1. $3\frac{1}{6}"+4\frac{1}{4}"+3\frac{5}{8}"+5\frac{7}{16}"+=3\frac{8}{48}"+4\frac{12}{48}"+3\frac{30}{48}"+5\frac{21}{48}"=15\frac{71}{48}"=16\frac{23}{48}"$

2. The flow of a 6" pipe is measured by the cross-sectional area. Since diameter = 6", radius = 3", and so area = 9π sq.in. A single 3" pipe would have a cross-sectional area of $(3/2)\pi$ sq.in. $= 2.25\pi$ sq.in. Now, $9 \div / 2.25 = 4$. Thus, four 3" pipes is equivalent, in flow, to one 6" pipe.

3. $(5 \times 4 \times 6) - (5 \times 4 \times 5\,1/2) = 10$. Then, $(10)(62) = 620$ pounds.

4. The total expansion $= (150')(.0000095"/1\text{ ft.})(190°-45°)$. So, the last factor is 145.

5. $(3')(50')(5\,1/2') = 825$ cu.ft. Since 1 cu.yd. = 27 cu.ft., 825 cu.ft. cu.yds.

6. $150 \div 20 = 7.5$. Then, $(7.5)(\$65) = \$487.50$

7. $(10')(3')(1/2') = 15$ cu.ft.

8. $4\frac{1}{16}+5\frac{4}{16}+3\frac{10}{16}+4\frac{7}{16}=16\frac{22}{16}=17\frac{3}{8}$

9. Gross salary $= (\$10.20)(40) + (\$15.30)(2) = \$438.60$

10. $75"=\frac{75}{100}"=\frac{3}{4}"$

11. 3 dozen = 36 shovels. Then, $36 \div 9 = 4$ weeks

12. Since 20% is deducted, the take-home pay $= (\$20,000)(.80) = \$16,000$ for the year, which is $\$16,000 \div 52 \approx \$308$ per week.

13. A scale drawing where 1/8" means an actual size of 1 ft. implies that a scale drawing of 1" means an actual size of $(1')(8) = 8'$

14. $(10')(12') = 120$ sq.ft. Since each tile is 1 sq.ft., a total of 120 tiles will be used.

15. $(30')(4')(1/4') = 30$ cu.ft.

16. To convert a given number of cubic feet into an equivalent number of cubic yards, divide by 27.

17. $5800 \div 50 = 116$ min. = 1 hour 56 minutes

18. $3\frac{1}{6}"+4\frac{1}{4}"+3\frac{5}{8}"+5\frac{7}{16}"+=3\frac{8}{48}"+4\frac{12}{48}"+3\frac{30}{48}"+5\frac{21}{48}"=15\frac{71}{48}"=16\frac{23}{48}"$

19. $2 \div 1/8 = 16$, so a 2" drawing represents an actual length of 16 feet.

20. The area of the 4 walls = 2(7 1/2')(8') + 2(9')(8') = 264 sq.ft. Then, 264 ÷ 400 = .66 or about 2/3 gallon of paint.

21. $3750 + $1200 + $3150 = $8100. Then, $3750/$8100 ≈ 46%

22. 2 cu.yds. ÷ 5 cu.ft. = 54 ÷ 5 = 10.8. Now, (10.8)(2 cu.ft.) ≈ 22 cu.ft. Note: 2 cu.yds. = 54 cu.ft.

23. (4)(6) = 24 man-days. Then, 24 ÷ 3 = 8 days

24. 2448 ÷ 144 = 17. Then, (17)($27.50) = $467.50

25. (75')(125') = 9375 sq.ft. The maximum area of the building = (.55)(9375 sq.ft.) * 5156 sq.ft.

TEST 3

Each question or incomplete statement is followed by several suggested answers or completions. Select the one that BEST answers the question or completes the statement. *PRINT THE LETTER OF THE CORRECT ANSWER IN THE SPACE AT THE RIGHT.*

1. A steak weighed 2 pounds, 4 ounces.
   How much did it cost at $4.60 per pound?　　　　　　　　　　　　　　　　1._____

   　A.　$7.80　　　　B.　$8.75　　　　C.　$9.90　　　　D.　$10.35

2. twenty pints of water just fill a pail.
   the capacity of the pail, in gallons, is　　　　　　　　　　　　　　　　2._____

   　A.　2　　　　　　B.　2 1/4　　　　C.　2 1/2　　　　D.　2 3/4

3. The sum of 5/12 and 1/4 is　　　　　　　　　　　　　　　　　　　　　3._____

   　A.　7/12　　　　B.　2/3　　　　　C.　3/4　　　　　D.　5/6

4. The volume of earth, in cubic yards, excavated from a trench 4'0" wide by 5'6" deep by　4._____
   18'6" long is MOST NEARLY

   　A.　14.7　　　　B.　15.1　　　　C.　15.5　　　　D.　15.9

5. 5/8 written as a decimal is　　　　　　　　　　　　　　　　　　　　　5._____

   　A.　62.5　　　　B.　6.25　　　　C.　.625　　　　D.　.0625

6. The number of cubic feet in a cubic yard is　　　　　　　　　　　　　　6._____

   　A.　9　　　　　　B.　12　　　　　C.　27　　　　　D.　36

7. If it costs $16.20 to lay one square yard of asphalt, to lay a patch 15' by 15', it will cost　7._____
   MOST NEARLY

   　A.　$405.00　　　B.　$3,645.00　　C.　$134.50　　　D.　$243.00

8. You are assigned thirty (30) asphalt workers to be divided into two crews so that one　8._____
   crew will have 2/3 as many men as the other.
   The number of men you would put into the SMALLER crew is

   　A.　10　　　　　B.　12　　　　　C.　14　　　　　D.　20

9. It takes 12 asphalt workers, working 6 hours a day, 5 days to complete a certain job.　9._____
   The number of days it will take 10 men, working 8 hours a day, to do the same job,
   assuming all work at the same rate, is.

   　A.　2 1/2　　　　B.　3　　　　　C.　4 1/2　　　　D.　6

0. A street is laid to a 3% grade.　　　　　　　　　　　　　　　　　　　10._____
   This means that in 150 ft., the street grade will rise

   　A.　4 1/2 inches　　　　　　　　　B.　45 inches
   　C.　4 1/2 feet　　　　　　　　　　D.　45 feet

11. The sum of the following dimensions, 3 4/8, 4 1/8, 5 1/8, and 6 1/4, is 11._____

    A. 19   B. 19 1/8   C. 19 1/4   D. 19 1/2

12. A worker is paid $9.30 per hour. 12._____
If he works 8 hours each day on Monday, Tuesday, and Wednesday, 3 1/2 hours on
Thursday, and 3 hours on Friday, the TOTAL amount due him is

    A. $283.65   B. $289.15   C. $276.20   D. $285.35

13. The price of metal lath is $395.00 per 100 square yards. The cost of 527 square yards of 13._____
this lath is MOST NEARLY

    A. $2,076.50   B. $2,079.10   C. $2,081.70   D. $2,084.30

14. The total cost of applying 221 square yards of plaster board is $3,430. 14._____
The cost per square yard is MOST NEARLY

    A. $14.00   B. $14.50   C. $15.00   D. $15.50

15. In a three-coat plaster job, the scratch coat is 1/8 in. thick in front of the lath, the brown 15._____
coat is 3/16 in. thick, and the finish coat is 1/8 in. thick.
The TOTAL thickness of this plaster job, measured from the face of the lath, is

    A. 7/16"   B. 1/2"   C. 9/16"   D. 5/8"

16. If an asphalt worker earns $38,070 per year, his wages per month are MOST NEARLY 16._____

    A. $380.70   B. $735.00   C. $3,170.00   D. $3,807.00

17. The sum of 4 1/2 inches, 3 1/4 inches, and 7 1/2 inches is 1 foot _____ inches. 17._____

    A. 3   B. 3 1/4   C. 3 1/2   D. 4

18. The area of a rectangular asphalt patch, 9 ft. 3 in. by 6 ft. 9 in., is _____square feet. 18._____

    A. 54   B. 54 1/4   C. 54 1/2   D. 62 7/16

19. The number of cubic feet in a cubic yard is 19._____

    A. 3   B. 9   C. 16   D. 27

20. A 450 ft. long street with a grade of 2% will have one end of the street higher than the 20._____
other end by _____ feet.

    A. 2   B. 44   C. 9   D. 20

21. If the drive wheel of a roller is 6 ft. in diameter and the tiller wheel is 4 ft. in diameter, 21._____
whenever the drive wheel makes a complete revolution on a straight pass, the tiller wheel
makes _____ revolution(s).

    A. 1   B. 1 1/4   C. 1 1/2   D. 2

22. A point on the centerline of a street is marked: Station 42 + 51. Another point on the cen- 22._____
terline 30 feet from the first is marked Station 42+81.
A third should be marked Station

    A. 12+51   B. 42+21   C. 45+51   D. 72+51

23. In twenty minutes, a truck moving with a speed of 30 miles an hour will cover a distance of _____ miles.   23._____

    A. 3   B. 5   C. 10   D. 30

24. The number of pounds in a ton is   24._____

    A. 500   B. 1,000   C. 2,000   D. 5,000

25. During his summer vacation, a boy earned $45.00 per day and saved 60% of his earnings.   25._____
If he worked 45 days, how much did he save during his vacation?

    A. $15.00   B. $18.00   C. $1,215.00   D. $22.50

KEY (CORRECT ANSWERS)

1.	D	11.	A
2.	C	12.	A
3.	B	13.	C
4.	B	14.	D
5.	C	15.	A
6.	C	16.	C
7.	A	17.	B
8.	B	18.	D
9.	C	19.	D
10.	C	20.	C

21.	C
22.	B
23.	C
24.	C
25.	C

SOLUTIONS TO PROBLEMS

1. ($4.60)(2 1/4 lbs.) = $10.35

2. 1 gallon = 8 pints, so 20 pints = 20/8 = 2 1/2 gallons

3. $\dfrac{5}{12}+\dfrac{1}{4}=\dfrac{5}{12}+\dfrac{3}{12}=\dfrac{8}{12}=\dfrac{2}{3}$

4. (4')(5 1/2')(18 1/2') = 407 cu.ft. Since 1 cu.yd. = 27 cu.ft., 407 cu.ft. $\approx$ 15.1 cu.yds.

5. 5/8=5 $\div$ 8.000 = .625

6. There are (3)(3)(3) =27 cu.ft. in a cu.yd.

7. (15')(15') = 225 sq.ft. = 25 sq.yds. Then, ($16.20)(25) = $405.00

8. Let 2x = size of smaller crew and 3x = size of larger crew. Then, 2x + 3x = 30. Solving, x = 6. Thus, the smaller crew consists of 12 workers.

9. (12)(6)(5) = 360 worker-days. Then, 360 $\div$ [(10)(8)] = 4 1/2 days

10. (.03)(150') = 4 1/2 ft.

11. $3\dfrac{4}{8}+4\dfrac{1}{8}+5\dfrac{1}{8}+6\dfrac{2}{8}=18\dfrac{8}{8}=19$

12. ($9.30)(8+8+8+3 1/2+3) = ($9.30)(30 1/2) = $283.65

13. The cost of 527 sq.yds. = (5.27)($395.00) = $2081.65 $\approx$ $2081.70

14. $3430 $\div$ 221 $\approx$ $15.50

15. $\dfrac{1}{8}"+\dfrac{3}{16}"+\dfrac{1}{8}"=\dfrac{2}{16}"+\dfrac{3}{16}"+\dfrac{2}{16}"=\dfrac{7}{16}"$

16. $38,070 $\div$ 12 = $3172.50 $\approx$ $3170.00 per month

17. 4 1/2" + 3 1/4" + 7 1/2" = 15 1/4" = 1 ft. 3 1/4 in.

18. 9 ft. 3 in. = 9 1/4 ft., 6 ft. 9 in. = 6 3/4 ft. Area = (9 1/4) (6 3/4) = 62 7/16 sq.ft.

19. A cubic yard = (3)(3)(3) = 27 cubic feet

20. (450')(.02) = 9 ft.

21. 6/4 = 1 1/2 revolutions

22. Station 42 + 51
    30 ft away would be 51 + 30 = 81 OR 51 - 30 = 21
    Station 42 + 81 or 42 + 21 (ANSWER: B)

23. 30 miles in 60 minutes means 10 miles in 20 minutes.

24. There are 2000 pounds in a ton.

25. ($45.00)(.60) = $27.00 savings per day. For 45 days, his savings is (45)($27.00) = $1215.00

———————

ARITHMETICAL REASONING
EXAMINATION SECTION
TEST 1

DIRECTIONS: Each question or incomplete statement is followed by several suggested
answers or completions. Select the one that BEST answers the question or
completes the statement. *PRINT THE LETTER OF THE CORRECT ANSWER
IN THE SPACE AT THE RIGHT.*

1. A supplier quotes a list price of $172.00 less 15 and 10 percent for twelve tools.   1.____
    The actual cost for these twelve tools is MOST NEARLY

    A. $146   B. $132   C. $129   D. $112

2. If the diameter of a circular piece of sheet metal is 1 1/2 feet, the area, in square inches,   2.____
    is MOST NEARLY

    A.   1.77   B.   2.36   C.   254   D.   324

3. The sum of 5'6", 7'3", 9'3 1/2", and 3'7 1/4" is   3.____

    A.   19'8 1/2"   B.   22' 1/2"   C.   25'7 3/4"   D.   28'8 3/4"

4. If the floor area of one shop is 15' by 21'3" and the size of an adjacent shop is 18' by   4.____
    30'6", then the TOTAL floor area of these two shops is _____ square feet.

    A.   1127.75   B.   867.75   C.   549.0   D.   318.75

5. The fraction which is equal to 0.875 is   5.____

    A.   7/16   B.   5/8   C.   3/4   D.   7/8

6. The sum of 1/2, 2 1/32, 4 3/16, and 1 7/8 is MOST NEARLY   6.____

    A.   9.593   B.   9.625   C.   9.687   D.   10.593

7. If the base of a right triangle is 9" and the altitude is 12", the length of the third side will be   7.____

    A.   13"   B.   14"   C.   15"   D.   16"

8. If a steel bar 1" in diameter and 12' long weighs 32 lbs., then the weight of a piece of this   8.____
    bar 5'9" long is MOST NEARLY _____ lbs.

    A.   15.33   B.   15.26   C.   16.33   D.   15.06

9. The diameter of a circle whose circumference is 12" is MOST NEARLY   9.____

    A.   3.82"   B.   3.72"   C.   3.62"   D.   3.52"

10. A dimension of 39/64 inches converted to decimals is MOST NEARLY   10.____

    A.   .600"   B.   .609"   C.   .607"   D.   .611"

11. A farm worker was paid a weekly wage of $415.20 for a 44-hour work week. As a result of a new labor contract, he is paid $431.40 a week for a 40-hour work week with time and one-half pay for time worked in excess of 40 hours in any work week.
If he continues to work 44 hours weekly under the new contract, the amount by which his average hourly rate for a 44-hour work week under the new contract exceeds the hourly rate previously paid him lies between _____ and _____, inclusive.

11.____

   A. 80¢; $1.00
   C. $1.25; $1.45
   B. $1.00; $1.20
   D. $1.50; $1.70

12. The sum of 4 feet 3 1/4 inches, 7 feet 2 1/2 inches, and 11 feet 1/4 inch is _____ feet _____ inches.

12.____

   A. 21; 6 1/4   B. 22; 6   C. 23; 5   D. 24; 5 3/4

13. The number 0.038 is read as

13.____

   A. 38 tenths
   C. 38 thousandths
   B. 38 hundredths
   D. 38 ten-thousandths

14. Assume that an employee is paid at the rate of $10.86 per hour with time and a half for overtime past 40 hours in a week.
If he works 43 hours in a week, his gross weekly pay is

14.____

   A. $434.40   B. $438.40   C. $459.18   D. $483.27

15. The sum of the following dimensions: 3'2 1/4", 8 7/8", 2'6 3/8", 2'9 3/4", and 1'0" is

15.____

   A. 16'7 1/4"   B. 10'7 1/4"   C. 10'3 1/4"   D. 9'3 1/4"

16. Two gears are meshed together and have a gear ratio of 6 to 1.
If the small gear rotates 120 revolutions per minute, the large gear rotates at

16.____

   A. 20   B. 40   C. 60   D. 720

17. The vacuum side of a compound gage reads 14 inches of vacuum. The barometer reading is 29.76 inches of mercury. The equivalent absolute pressure of the compound gage reading, in inches of mercury, is MOST likely

17.____

   A. 15.06   B. 15.76   C. 43.06   D. 43.76

18. The fraction 5/8 expressed as a decimal is

18.____

   A. 0.125   B. 0.412   C. 0.625   D. 0.875

19. If 300 feet of a certain size pipe weighs 450 pounds, the number of pounds that 100 feet will weigh is

19.____

   A. 1,350   B. 150   C. 300   D. 250

20. As an oiler, you work for a facility that has automobiles that use, on the average, 600 quarts of one grade of lubricating oil every month.
The number of one-gallon cans of the above oil that should be ordered each month to meet this requirement is

20.____

   A. 100   B. 125   C. 140   D. 150

21. The inside dimensions of a rectangular oil gravity tank are: height 15", width 9", length 10".
The amount of oil in the tank, in gallons, (231 cu.in. = 1 gallon), when the oil level is 9" high, is MOST NEARLY

21.____

    A.   2.3   B.   3.5   C.   5.2   D.   5.8

22. If 30 gallons of oil cost $76.80, 45 gallons of oil at the same rate will cost

22.____

    A. $91.20   B. $115.20   C. $123.20   D. $131.20

23. If an oiler earns $18,000 in the first six months of a year and receives a 10% raise in salary for the next six months of the same year, his TOTAL earnings for the year will be

23.____

    A. $36,000   B. $37,500   C. $37,800   D. $39,600

24. If the cost of lubricating oil increases 15%, then a gallon of oil which used to cost $10.00 will now cost MOST NEARLY

24.____

    A. $10.50   B. $11.00   C. $11.50   D. $12.00

25. The sum of 7/8", 3/4", 1/2", and 3/8" is

25.____

    A.   2 1/8"   B.   2 1/4"   C.   2 3/8"   D.   2 1/2"

KEY (CORRECT ANSWERS)

1.	B		11.	A
2.	C		12.	B
3.	C		13.	C
4.	B		14.	D
5.	D		15.	C
6.	A		16.	A
7.	C		17.	B
8.	A		18.	C
9.	A		19.	B
10.	B		20.	D

21.	B
22.	B
23.	C
24.	C
25.	D

SOLUTIONS TO PROBLEMS

1. Actual cost = ($172)(,85)(.90) = $131.58 ≈ $132

2. Radius = .75', then area = (3.14)(.75)^2 ≈ 1.77 sq.ft.
   Since 1 sq.ft. = 144 sq.in., the area ≈ 254 sq.in.

3. 5'6" + 7'3" + 9'3 1/2" + 3'7 1/4" = 24'19 3/4" = 25'7 3/4"

4. Total area = (15)(21.25) + (18)(30.5) = 867.75 sq.ft.

5. .875 = 875/1000 = 7/8

6. 1 1/2 + 2 1/32 + 4 3/16 + 1 7/8 = 8 51/32 = 9 19/32 = 9.593

7. Third side = $\sqrt{9^2+12^2} = \sqrt{225} = 15"$

8. Let x = weight. Then, 12/32 = 5.75/x . Solving, x ≈ 15.33 lbs.

9. 12" = (3.14)(diameter), so diameter ≈ 3.82"

10. $\frac{39}{64}$" = .609375" ≈ .609"

11. Under his new contract, the weekly wage for 44 hours can be found by first determining his hourly rate for the first 40 hours = $431.40 ÷ 40 ≈ $10.80. Now, his time and one-half pay will = ($10.80)(1.5) = $16.20. His weekly wage for the new contract = $431.40 + (4)($16.20) = $496,20. His new hourly rate for 44 hours = $496.20 ÷ 44 ≈ $10.34. Under the old contract, his hourly rate for 44 hours was $415.20 ÷ 44 = $9.44. His hourly rate increase = $10.34 - $9.44 = $0.90. (Answer key: between $0.80 and $1.00)

12. 4'3 1/4" + 7'2 1/2" + 11' 1/4" = 22'6"

13. .038 = 38 thousandths

14. ($10.86)(40) + ($16.29)(3) = $483.27

15. 3'2 1/4" + 8 7/8" + 2'6 3/8" + 2'9 3/4" + 1'0" = 8'25 18/8" = 10'3 1/4"

16. The gear ratio is inversely proportional to the gear size. Let x = large gear's rpm. Then, 6/1 = 120/x . Solving, x = 20

17. Subtract 14 from 29.76

18. 5/8 = .625

19. Let x = number of pounds. Then, 300/450 = 100/x . Solving, x = 150

20. 600 quarts = 150 gallons, since 4 quarts = 1 gallon

21. (9")(9")(10") = 810 cu.in. Then, 810 ÷ 231 ≈ 3.5

22. Let x = unknown cost. Then, 30/$76.80 = 45/x. Solving, x = $115.20

23. $18,000 + ($18,000)(1.10) = $37,800

24. ($10.00)(1.15) = $11.50

25. 7/8" + 3/4" + 1/2" + 3/8" = 20/8" = 2 1/2"

TEST 2

DIRECTIONS: Each question or incomplete statement is followed by several suggested answers or completions. Select the one that BEST answers the question or completes the statement. *PRINT THE LETTER OF THE CORRECT ANSWER IN THE SPACE AT THE RIGHT.*

1. A sheet metal plate has been cut in the form of a right triangle with sides of 5, 12, and 13 inches.
    The area of this plate, in square inches, is

    A. 30　　　　B. 32 1/2　　　　C. 60　　　　D. 78

    1.____

2. If steel weighs 480 lbs. per cubic foot, the weight of an 18" x 18" x 2" steel base plate is _____ lbs.

    A. 180　　　　B. 216　　　　C. 427　　　　D. 648

    2.____

3. By trial, it is found that by using 2 cubic feet of sand, a 5 cubic foot batch of concrete is produced.
    Using the same proportions, the amount of sand, in cubic feet, required to produce 2 cubic yards of concrete is MOST NEARLY

    A. 7　　　　B. 22　　　　C. 27　　　　D. 45

    3.____

4. The total number of cubic yards of earth to be removed to make a trench 3'9" wide, 25'0" long, and 4'3" deep is MOST NEARLY

    A. 53.1　　　　B. 35.4　　　　C. 26.6　　　　D. 14.8

    4.____

5. A large number of 2 x 4 studs, some 10'5" long and some 6'5 1/2" long, are required for a job.
    To minimize waste, it would be PREFERABLE to order lengths of _____ feet.

    A. 16　　　　B. 17　　　　C. 18　　　　D. 19

    5.____

6. A 6" pipe is connected to a 4" pipe through a reducer. If 100 cubic feet of water is flowing through the 6" pipe per minute, the flow, in cubic feet, per minute through the 4" pipe is

    A. 225　　　　B. 100　　　　C. 66.6　　　　D. 44.4

    6.____

7. If steel weighs 0.28 pounds per cubic inch, then the weight, in pounds, of a 2" square steel bar 120" long is MOST NEARLY

    A. 115　　　　B. 125　　　　C. 135　　　　D. 155

    7.____

8. A three-inch diameter steel bar two feet long weighs MOST NEARLY (assume steel weighs 480 lbs./cu.ft.) _____ lbs.

    A. 48　　　　B. 58　　　　C. 68　　　　D. 78

    8.____

9. The area of a circular plate will be reduced by 5% if a sector removed from it has an angle of _____ degrees.

    A. 18　　　　B. 24　　　　C. 32　　　　D. 60

    9.____

10. If a 4 1/16 inch shaft wears six thousandths of an inch, the NEW diameter will be _____ inches.   10._____

     A.   4.0031   B.   4.0565   C.   4.0578   D.   4.0605

11. A set of mechanical plan drawings is drawn to a scale of 1/8" = 1 foot. If a length of pipe measures 15 7/16" on the drawing, the ACTUAL length of the pipe is _____ feet.   11._____

     A.   121.5   B.   122.5   C.   123.5   D.   124.5

12. An electrical drawing is drawn to a scale of 1/4" = 1'. If a length of conduit on the drawing measures 7 3/8", the actual length of the conduit, in feet, is   12._____

     A.   7.5   B.   15.5   C.   22.5   D.   29.5

13. Assume that you have assigned 6 mechanics to do a job that must be finished in 4 days. At the end of 3 days, your men have completed only two-thirds of the job. In order to complete the job on time and because the job is such that it cannot be speeded up, you should assign a MINIMUM of _____ extra men.   13._____

     A.   3   B.   4   C.   5   D.   6

14. Assume that a trench is 42" wide, 5' deep, and 100' long. If the unit price of excavating the trench is $105 per cubic yard, the cost of excavating the trench is MOST NEARLY   14._____

     A. $6,805   B. $15,330   C. $21,000   D. $63,000

15. If the scale on a shop drawing is 1/4 inch to the foot, then the length of a part which measures 2 3/8 inches long on the drawing is ACTUALLY _____ feet.   15._____

     A.   9 1/2   B.   8 1/2   C.   7 1/4   D.   4 1/4

16. It is necessary to pour a new concrete floor for a shop. If the dimensions of the concrete slab for the floor are to be 27' x 18' x 6", then the number of cubic yards of concrete that must be poured is   16._____

     A.   9   B.   16   C.   54   D.   243

17. The jaws of a vise move 1/4" for each complete turn of the handle. The number of complete turns necessary to open the jaws 2 3/4" is   17._____

     A.   9   B.   10   C.   11   D.   12

18. Assume that a jobbing shop is to submit a price for a contract involving 300 pieces of work. Assume that material costs 50 cents per piece, labor costs $7.50 an hour, and a lathe operator can complete 5 pieces in an hour.
If overhead is 40% of material and labor costs and the profit is 10% of all costs, the submitted price for the entire job will be   18._____

     A. $630.24   B. $872.80   C. $900.00   D. $924.00

19. The following formula is used in connection with the three-wire method of measuring pitch diameters of screw threads: $G = \dfrac{0.57735}{N}$, where G = wire size and N = number of threads per inch.

    According to this formula, the proper size of wire for a 1"-8NC thread is MOST NEARLY

    A. .0722"   B. .7217"   C. .0072"   D. .0074"   19._____

20. A millimeter is 1/25.4 of an inch and there are 10 millimeters to a centimeter. If a piece of stock measures 127 centimeters long, the length of the stock, in feet and inches, would be MOST NEARLY

    A. 2'1"   B. 4'2"   C. 8'4"   D. 41'8"   20._____

21. For a certain job, you will need 25 steel bars 1 inch in diameter and 4"6" long. If these bars weigh 3 pounds per foot of length, then the TOTAL weight for all 25 bars is _____ pounds.

    A. 13.5   B. 75.0   C. 112.5   D. 337.5   21._____

22. If steel weighs 0.30 pounds per cubic inch, then the weight of a 2 inch square steel bar 90 inches long is _____ pounds.

    A. 27   B. 54   C. 108   D. 360   22._____

23. A concrete wall is 36' long, 9' high, and 1 1/2' thick. The number of cubic yards of concrete that were needed to make this wall is

    A. 14   B. 18   C. 27   D. 36   23._____

24. If the scale on a shop drawing is 1/2 inch to the foot, then the length of a part which measures 41/4 inches long on the drawing has a length of APPROXIMATELY _____ feet.

    A. 2 1/8   B. 4 1/4   C. 8 1/2   D. 10 3/4   24._____

25. If the allowable load on a wooden scaffold is 60 pounds per square foot and the scaffold surface area is 3 feet by 12 feet, then the MAXIMUM total distributed load that is permitted on the scaffold is _____ pounds.

    A. 720   B. 1,800   C. 2,160   D. 2,400   25._____

KEY (CORRECT ANSWERS)

1.	A	11.	C
2.	A	12.	D
3.	B	13.	A
4.	D	14.	A
5.	B	15.	A
6.	B	16.	A
7.	C	17.	C
8.	A	18.	D
9.	A	19.	A
10.	B	20.	B

21.	D
22.	C
23.	B
24.	C
25.	C

SOLUTIONS TO PROBLEMS

1. Area = (1/2)(base)(height) = (1/2)(5")(12") = 30 sq.in.

2. Volume = (18") (18") (2") = 648 cu.in. = 648/1720 cu.ft.
    Then, (480)(648/1720) = $\approx$ 180 lbs.

3. 2 cu.yds. = 54 cu.ft. Let x = required cubic feet of sand. Then, 2/5 = x/54. Solving, x = 21.6 (or about 22)

4. (3.75')(25')(4.25') = 398.4375 cu.ft. $\approx$ 14.8 cu.yds.

5. 10'5" + 6'5 1/2" = 16'10 1/2", so lengths of 17 feet are needed

6. The amount of water flowing through each pipe must be equal.

7. (2")(2")(120") = 480 cu. in. Then, (480)(.28) $\approx$ 135 lbs.

8. Volume = (π) (.125 ')^2 (2) $\approx$ .1 cu.ft. Then, (.1)(480) = 48 lbs.

9. (360°)(.05) - 18°

10. 4 1/16 - .006 = 4.0625 - .006 = 4.0565

11. 15 7/16" $\div$ 1/8" = 247/16 . 8/1 = 123.5. Then, (123.5)(1 ft.) = 123.5 ft.

12. 7 3/8" $\div$ 1/4" = 59/8 . 4/1 = 29.5   Then, (29.5)(1 ft.) = 29.5 ft.

13. (6)(4) = 24 man-days normally required. Since after 3 days only the equivalent of (2/3)(24) = 16 man-days of work has been 1 done, 8 man-days of work is still left. 16 $\div$ 3 = 5 1/3, which means the crew is equivalent to only 5 1/3 men. To do the 8 man-days of work, it will require at least 8 - 5 1/3 = 2 2/3 = 3 additional men.

14. (3.5')(5')(100') = 1750 cu.ft. $\approx$ 64.8 cu.yds. Then, (64.8)($105) $\approx$ $6805

15. 2 3/8" $\div$ 1/4" = 19/8 . 4/1 = 9 1/2 Then, (9 1/2)(1 ft.) = 9 1/2 feet

16. (27')(18')(1/2') = 243 cu.ft. = 9 cu.yds. (1 cu.yd. = 27 cu.ft.)

17. 2 3/4" $\div$ 1/4" = 11/4 . 4/1 = 11

18. Material cost = (300)($.50) = $150. Labor cost = ($7.50)(300/5) = $450. Overhead = (.40)($150+$450) = $240. Profit = .10($150+$450+$240) = $84. Submitted price = $150 + $450 + $240 + $84 = $924

19. 6 = .57735" $\div$ 8 = .0722"

20.　127 cm = 1270 mm = 1270/25.4" $\approx$ 50" = 4.2"

21.　(25)(4.5') = 112.5' Then, (112.5X3) = 337.5 lbs.

22.　(2")(2")(90") = 360 cu.in. Then, (360)(30) = 108 lbs.

23.　(36')(9')(1 1/2') = 486 cu.ft. = 18 cu.yds. (1 cu.yd. = 27 cu.ft.)

24.　4 1/4" ÷ 1/2" = 17/4 . 2/1 = 8 1/2. Then, (8 1/2)(1 ft.) = 8 1/2 ft.

25.　(12')(3') = 36 sq.ft. Then, (36)(60) = 2160 lbs.

————————

TEST 3

DIRECTIONS: Each question or incomplete statement is followed by several suggested answers or completions. Select the one that BEST answers the question or completes the statement. *PRINT THE LETTER OF THE CORRECT ANSWER IN THE SPACE AT THE RIGHT.*

1. A right triangular metal sheet for a roofing job has sides of 36 inches and 4 feet. The length of the remaining side is

   A. 7 feet
   C. 60 inches
   B. 6 feet
   D. 90 inches

   1.____

2. A U.S. Standard Gauge thickness is given as 0.15625. This thickness, in fractions of an inch, is MOST NEARLY _____ inches.

   A. 1/8   B. 4/32   C. 5/32   D. 3/64

   2.____

3. The weight per 100 of sheet metal fasteners is given as 2/3 pound. The APPROXIMATE number of fasteners in a 2-pound package is

   A. 166   B. 200   C. 300   D. 266

   3.____

4. The decimal equivalent of 27/32 is MOST NEARLY

   A. 0.813   B. 0.828   C. 0.844   D. 0.859

   4.____

5. If a scaled measurement of 1'3" on the drawing of a sheet metal layout represents an actual length of 10"0", then the drawing has been made to a scale of _____ inch to the foot.

   A. 3/4   B. 1 1/4   C. 1 1/2   D. 1 3/4

   5.____

6. Two and two-thirds tees can be made from one sheet of steel. If 24 tees must be made, then the number of sheets required is

   A. 6   B. 7   C. 8   D. 9

   6.____

7. A main duct 20 inches in diameter discharges into two branch ducts. The sum of the areas of the branches is to be equal to the area of the main duct. One branch is 12 inches in diameter.
   The diameter of the other branch is _____ inches.

   A. 16   B. 12   C. 10   D. 8

   7.____

8. If steel weighs 480 lbs. per cubic foot, the weight of 10 sheets, each 6 feet by 3 feet by 1/32 inch, is _____ lbs.

   A. 2,700   B. 1,237   C. 270   D. 225

   8.____

9. The area, in square inches, of a right triangle that has sides of 12 1/2, 10, and 7 1/2 inches is

   A. 18 1/4   B. 37 1/2   C. 75   D. 60

   9.____

10. In making a container to hold 1 gallon (231 cu.in.) and to be 6 inches in diameter at the top and 8 inches in diameter at the bottom, the height must be, in inches,

    A. 10.0   B. 8.2   C. 4.6   D. 6

10.____

11. A sheet metal worker is given a job to make a transition piece from a 8 1/2" diameter duct to an 11 1/4" diameter duct. If the length of the transition piece is 5 1/2" for each inch change in diameter, then the length of the transition piece is

    A. 14 7/8"   B. 15"   C. 15 1/8"   D. 15 1/4"

11.____

12. A duct layout is drawn to a scale of 3/8" to a foot. If the length of a run shown on the drawing scales 7 1/2", then the ACTUAL length of the run is

    A. 19'6"   B. 19'9"   C. 20'0"   D. 20'3"

12.____

13. An 18" x 24" duct is to be connected to a 24" x 24" duct by means of an eccentric transition piece (3 sides flush). If the taper is to be 1" in 4", then the length of the transition piece is

    A. 6"   B. 12"   C. 18"   D. 24"

13.____

14. Twenty-seven pairs of 3/8" diameter rods each 3'3 1/2" long are needed to support a duct.
If the available rods are ten feet long, then the MINIMUM number of rods that will be needed to make the twenty-seven sets is

    A. 9   B. 12   C. 15   D. 18

14.____

15. A rectangular sheet metal air duct with open ends is 12 feet long and 15" x 20" in cross-section. If one square foot of the sheet metal weighs 1/2 pound, then the TOTAL weight of the duct is _____ lbs.

    A. 10   B. 17 1/2   C. 35   D. 150

15.____

16. The sum of 1/12 and 1/4 is

    A. 1/3   B. 5/12   C. 7/12   D. 3/8

16.____

17. The product of 12 and 2 1/3 is

    A. 27   B. 28   C. 29   D. 30

17.____

18. If 4 1/2 is subtracted from 7 1/5, the remainder is

    A. 3 7/10   B. 2 7/10   C. 3 3/10   D. 2 3/10

18.____

19. The number of cubic yards in 47 cubic feet is MOST NEARLY

    A. 1.70   B. 1.74   C. 1.78   D. 1.82

19.____

20. A wall 8'0" high by 12'6" long has a window opening 4'0" high by 3'6" wide. The net area of the wall (allowing for the window opening) is, in square feet,

    A. 86   B. 87   C. 88   D. 89

20.____

21. A worker's hourly rate is $11.36.
    If he works 11 1/2 hours, he should receive

    A. $129.84   B. $130.64   C. $131.48   D. $132.24

21.____

22. The number of cubic feet in 3 cubic yards is

    A. 81   B. 82   C. 83   D. 84

22.____

23. At an annual rate of $.40 per $100, what is the fire insurance premium for one year on a house that is insured for $80,000?

    A. $120   B. $160   C. $240   D. $320

23.____

24. A meter equals approximately 1.09 yards.
    How much longer, in yards, is a 100-meter dash than a 100-yard dash?

    A. 6   B. 8   C. 9   D. 12

24.____

25. A train leaves New York City at 8:10 A.M. and arrives in Buffalo at 4:45 P.M. on the same day. How long, in hours and minutes, does it take the train to make the trip?
    _____ hours, _____ minutes.

    A. 6; 22   B. 7; 16   C. 7; 28   D. 8; 35

25.____

_____

KEY (CORRECT ANSWERS)

1. C		11. C	
2. C		12. C	
3. C		13. D	
4. C		14. D	
5. C		15. C	
6. D		16. A	
7. A		17. B	
8. D		18. B	
9. B		19. B	
10. D		20. A	

21. B
22. A
23. D
24. C
25. D

_____

SOLUTIONS TO PROBLEMS

1. Let x = remaining side. Converting to inches, $x^2 = 36^2 + 48^2$ So, $x^2 = 3600$. Solving, $x = 60$ inches.

2. $.15625 = \dfrac{15,625}{100,000} = \dfrac{5}{32}$

3. $2 \div 2/3 = 3$. Then, $(3)(100) = 300$ fasteners

4. $27/32 = .84375 \approx .844$

5. $1'3" \div 10 = 15" \div 10 = 1\ 1/2"$

6. $24 \div 2\ 2/3 = 24/1.3/8 = 9$

7. Area of main duct = $(\pi)(10^2) = 100\,\pi$. One of the branches has an area of $(\pi)(6^2) = 36\,\pi$. Thus, the area of the 2nd branch = $100\,\pi - 36\,\pi = 64\,\pi$. The 2nd branch's radius must be 8" and its diameter must be 16".

8. Volume = $(1/384')(6')(3') = .046875$ cu.ft. Then, 10 sheets have a volume of .46875 cu.ft. Now, $(.46875)(480) = 225$ lbs.

9. Note that $(7\ 1/2)^2 + (10)^2 = (12\ 1/2)^2$, so that this is a right triangle. Area = $(1/2)(10")(7\ 1/2")$ = 371/2 sq.in.

10. $231 = \dfrac{h}{3}[(\pi)(3)^2 + (\pi)(4)^2 + \sqrt{(9\pi)(16\pi)}],$ where h = required height. Then,

    $231 = \dfrac{h}{3}(9\pi + 16\pi + 12\pi).$ Simplifying, $231 = 37\,\pi\,h/3$.
    Solving, h ~ 5.96" or 6"

11. $11\ 1/4 - 8\ 1/2 = 2\ 3/4$. Then, $(2\ 3/4)(5\ 1/2) = 11/4 .11/2 = 15\ 1/8$

12. $7\ 1/2\ " \div 3/8" = 15/2 .8/3 = 20$ Then, $(20)(1\ \text{ft.}) = 20$ feet

13. $24" - 18" = 6"$ Then, $(6")(4) = 24"$

14. $3'3\ 1/2" = 39.5"$. Now, $(27)(2)(39.5") = 2133"$. 10 ft. = 120".
    Finally, $2133 \div 120 = 17.775$, so 18 rods are needed.

15. Surface area = $(2)(12')(1\ 1/4') + (2)(12')(1\ 2/3') = 70$ sq.ft.
    Then, $(70)(1/2\ \text{lb.}) - 35$ lbs.

16. $1/12 + 1/4 = 4/12 = 1/3$

17. (12)(2 1/3) = 12/1 . 7/3 = 28

18. 7 1/5 - 4 1/2 = 7 2/10 - 4 5/10 = 6 12/10 - 4 5/10 = 2 7/10

19. 47 cu.ft. = 47/27 cu.yds. = 1.74 cu.yds.

20. (8')(12.5') - (4')(3.5') = 86 sq.ft.

21. ($11.36)(11.5) = $130.64

22. 1 cu.yd. = 27 cu.ft., so 3 cu.yds. = 81 cu.ft.

23. $80,000 ÷ $100 = 800. Then, (800)($.40) = $320

24. 100 meters = 109 yds. Then, 109 - 100 = 9 yds.

25. 4:45 P.M. - 8:10 AM. = 8 hrs. 35 min.

_____

MATHEMATICS PROBLEM SOLVING

EXAMINATION SECTION
TEST 1

COMMENTARY

Perhaps the supreme factor or criterion in measuring and evaluating the applicant's (candidate's) ability to reason is the problem-solving question frequently used, on one or more levels of difficulty, in tests of general and mental ability, aptitude, achievement, etc.

There follow, in graded sequence, several tests of problem-solving, together with answers.

SAMPLE QUESTIONS AND SOLUTIONS

SAMPLE QUESTION 1
If 1 lb. of tea costs 75¢, what will 5 lbs. cost?
The answer required consists of a number of cents; also, the more lbs., the *more* cents.
Since the number of cents which 1 lb. costs is 75, therefore, the number of cents which 5 lbs. cost is 5 times 75, that is, 375 (cents) or $3.75.

SAMPLE QUESTION 2
If 12 horses can plough 75 acres in a certain time, how many acres can 28 horses plough in the same time?
The answer required consists of a number of acres; also, the more horses, the *more* acres.
Since the number of acres which 12 horses plough is 75, therefore, the number of acres which 1 horse can plough is 1/12 of 75, and the number of acres which 28 horses can plough is 28 times 1/12 of 75, that is, 175 (acres).

QUESTIONS

1. If 1 lb. of sugar costs 60¢, *how much* will 11 lbs. of the same sugar cost?   1.____

2. If 8 lbs. of coffee cost $32.00, *how much* will 1 lb. of the same coffee cost?   2.____

3. If 4 lbs. of sugar cost $2.40, *how much* will 14 lbs. cost?   3.____

4. If the railway fare for 96 miles is $28.80, what is the railway fare for 1 mile; for 20 miles?   4.____

5. If it costs $100 to send 8 tons a certain distance, *how much* will it cost to send 10 tons the same distance? 5.____

6. If it takes 6 hours to pump 5400 gallons of water with a certain pump, *how many* gallons can be pumped in 1 hour? How many can be pumped in 7 hours?   6.____

7. If 20 men can reap 15 acres in one day, *how many* acres can 32 men reap in one day?   7.____

8. If 8 horses can plough 56 acres in a certain time, *how many* acres can 11 horses plough in the same time?   8.____

9. A man walks 65 miles in 13 hours; in *how many* hours will he walk 45 miles at the same pace?   9.____

10. If 840 widgets weigh 21 lbs., *how many* lbs. will 480 widgets weigh?   10.____

————

KEY (CORRECT ANSWERS)

1.	$6.60	6.	(i) 900;
2.	$4.00		(ii) 6300
3.	$8.40	7.	24 acres
4.	30¢; $6.00	8.	77 acres
5.	$125	9.	9 hrs.
		10.	12 lbs.

————

TEST 2

SAMPLE QUESTION 1

If 9 men do a piece of work in 7 days, in how many days will 1 man do the same?

The answer consists of a number of days; also, the fewer men, the *more* days.

Since the number of days in which 9 men can do the work is 7, therefore the number of days in which 1 man can do the work is 9 times 7, that is, 63 (days).

SAMPLE QUESTION 2

If 9 men can do a piece of work in 20 days, how many men could do it in 15 days?

The answer required is a number of men; also, the more days, the *fewer* men. Since the number of men who do the work in 20 days

is 9, therefore, the number of men who could do it in 1 day is 20 times 9, and the number

of men who could do it in 15 days is 1/15 of 20 times 9, that is, $\dfrac{5 \times 4 \times 3 \times 3}{5 \times 3}$ or 12 (men)

QUESTIONS

1. If 7 men can mow a field in 3 days, in *how many* days could 1 man mow the same field?   1.____

2. A ship performs a voyage in 75 days, sailing 5 knots an hour; *how many* days would she take to perform the same voyage sailing 1 knot an hour?   2.____

3. If 5 horses can plough a field in 7 days, in *how many* days could 7 horses plough the same field?   3.____

4. A man walks from a certain distance in 14 hours, walking 4 miles an hour; *how long* would he take if he rode at the rate of 7 miles an hour?   4.____

5. A train performs a journey in 7 hours, travelling at the rate of 35 miles an hour; *how long* would it take to do the same distance, travelling at the rate of 49 miles an hour?   5.____

6. A garrison of 2500 men has provisions for 11 months; *how long* would they last if the garrison were reduced to 100 men?   6.____

7. If 12 men can mow a field in 22 days, *how long* would 33 men take to mow the same field?   7.____

8. In *what time* will 39 men do a piece of work, which it takes 30 men 26 days to accomplish?   8.____

9. If 20 bushels of corn feed 24 horses for 15 days, for *how many* days will they feed 9 horses?   9.____

10. If 18 horses plough 111 1/2 acres in 15 days, *how many* horses can plough the same number of acres in 27 days?   10.____

_____

KEY (CORRECT ANSWERS)

1. 21 days
2. 375 days
3. 5 days
4. 8 hours
5. 5 hours

6. 275 mtbs.
7. 8 d.
8. 20 d.
9. 40
10. 10

———

TEST 3

SAMPLE QUESTION 1

If a loaf at 12¢ weighs 64 oz. when wheat is $13.50 per quarter, what should it weigh when wheat is $18 per quarter?

The answer required is a number of ounces; also, the more dollars per qr., the fewer the number of oz.

Since the number of oz. when wheat is $13.50 per qr. is 64, therefore, the number of oz. when wheat is $1 per qr. is 13 1/2 x 64, and the number of oz. when wheat is $18 per qr.

is $\dfrac{13\frac{1}{2}}{18} \times 64$ is 48 (oz.)

SAMPLE QUESTION 2

If 75 bushels feed 27 horses for a week, how many horses will 125 bushels feed for the same time?

The answer required is a number of horses; also, the more bushels, the more horses.

Since the number of horses fed by 75 bushels is 27, therefore, the number of horses fed by 1 bushel is 1/75 of 27, and the number of Horses fed by 125 bushels is 125/76 of 27, or 45 (horses).

QUESTIONS

1. If a workman earns $100 in 50 working days, *how many* days will he take to earn $210? 1.____

2. If 12 men reap a field in 20 hours, in *how many* hours will 16 men reap the same field? 2.____

3. If a carriage of 3 cwt. for 72 miles cost a certain sum, *how much* will be carried 27 miles for the same money? 3.____

4. If a 2-cent loaf weighs 10 oz. when wheat is $3 per bushel, *what* is the price per bushel when a 2-cent loaf weighs 6 oz.? 4.____

5. If the rent of 42 acres of land is $1260, *how many* acres of the same land should be let for $810? 5.____

6. If 13 cwt. cost $169, *what* will 50 cwt. cost? 6.____

7. How many men can do a piece of work in 16 hrs. when 4 men can do in 24 hrs.? 7.____

8. In *how many* days can 20 men do a piece of work which it takes 125 men to do in 64 days? 8.____

9. If, from a sack of flour, a baker can make 48 loaves weighing 3 lbs. each, *how many* 4-lb. loaves can he make from the same? 9.____

10. If 40 bushels feed 60 horses for a week, *how many* horses would they keep for 35 days? 10.____

11. If 40 bushels feed 60 horses for a week, *how many* bushels will be required to feed 27 horses for the same time? 11.____

12. If 40 bushels feed 60 horses for a week, for *how many* days would they feed 12 horses? 12.____

13. If 40 bushels feed 60 horses for a week, for *how many* days would 280 bushels feed the same number of horses? 13.____

14. If 40 bushels feed 60 horses for a week, *how many* will be required to feed the same number of horses for 35 days? 14.____

15. *How many* yards of cloth worth $1.25 per yard must be given for 35 yards at $1.75 per yard? 15.____

16. If for the loan of a sum of money for 5 months, I pay $221, what would I to pay for a year? 16.____

17. If 63 yds. of cloth cost $225, *how many* yds. cost $150? 17.____

18. A certain amount of sugar costs $168 at 7¢ per lb. , *how much* will it cost at 8¢ per lb.? 18.____

19. A certain amount of sugar costs $168 at 7¢ per lb. , *how much* will it cost at 8¢ per lb.? 19.____

20. A bankrupt pays $3 in every $5, and his assets are $2250; *what* are his debts? 20.____

———

KEY (CORRECT ANSWERS)

1.	105 days	11.	18 bus.
2.	15 hrs.	12.	35 days
3.	8 cwt.	13.	49 days
4.	$5	14.	200 bus.
5.	27 acres	15.	49 yds.
6.	$650	16.	$530.40
7.	6 men	17.	42 yds.
8.	400 days	18.	$192
9.	36 loaves	19.	$2800
10.	12 horses	20.	$3750

———

EXAMINATION SECTION
TEST 1

DIRECTIONS: Each question or incomplete statement is followed by two suggested answers or completions. Select A or B, or C if the two figures have the same value, as the BEST answer that completes the statement or completes the statement. *PRINT THE LETTER OF THE CORRECT ANSWER IN THE SPACE AT THE RIGHT.*

1.

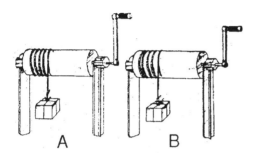

With which windlass can a man raise the heavier weight?

1.____

2.

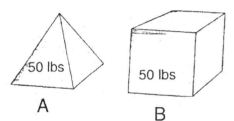

Which of these solid blocks will be the harder to tip over?

2.____

3.

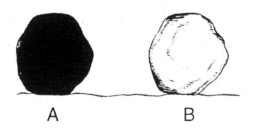

Which rock will get hotter in the sun?

3.____

4.

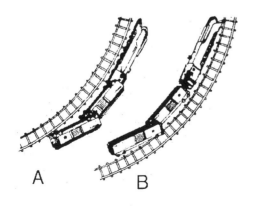

Which of these is the more likely picture of a train wreck?

4.____

5.

If the track is exactly level, on which rail does more pressure come?

5.____

6.

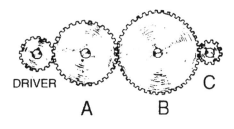

Which picture shows the way a bomb falls from a moving airplane if there is no wind?

6.____

7.

Indicate a gear which turn the same direction as the driver.

7.____

8.

If there are no clouds, on which night will you be able to see more stars?

8.____

9.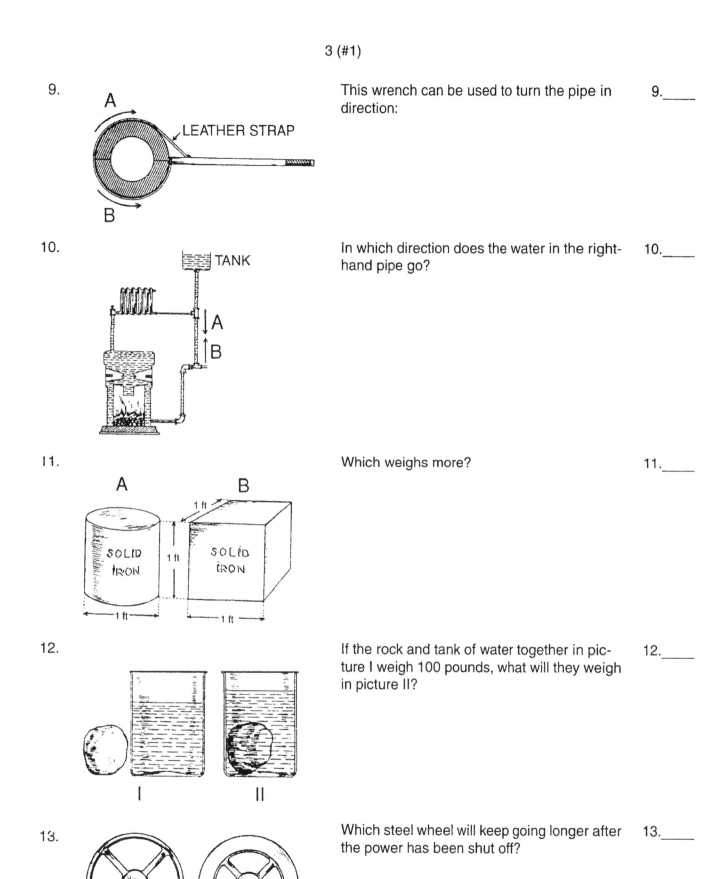

This wrench can be used to turn the pipe in direction:

9.____

10.

In which direction does the water in the right-hand pipe go?

10.____

11.

Which weighs more?

11.____

12.

If the rock and tank of water together in picture I weigh 100 pounds, what will they weigh in picture II?

12.____

13.

Which steel wheel will keep going longer after the power has been shut off?

13.____

14.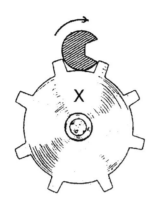

The top of the wheel *X* will go

    A.   steadily to the right
    B.   steadily to the left
    C.   by jerks to the left

14.____

15.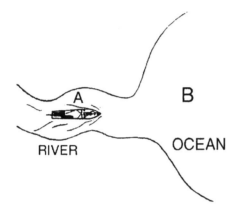

At which point will the boat be lower in the water?

15.____

16.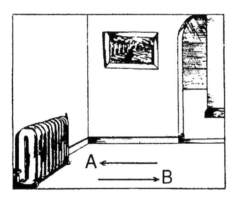

Which arrow shows the way the air will move along the floor when the radiator is turned on?

16.____

17.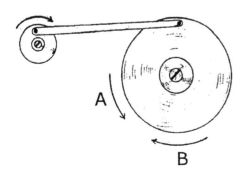

When the little wheel turns around, the big wheel will

    A.   turn in direction A
    B.   turn in direction B
    C.   move back and forth

17.____

18.

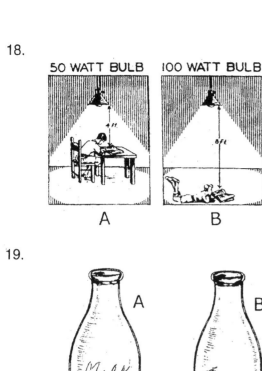

50 WATT BULB   100 WATT BULB

A   B

Which boy gets more light on the pages of his book?   18.____

19.

Which weighs more?   19.____

20.

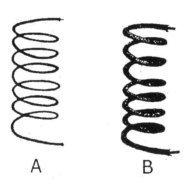

A   B

Which of these wires offers more resistance to the passage of an electric current?   20.____

21.

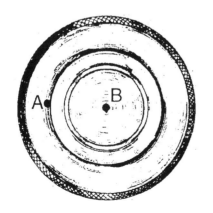

Which spot on the wheel travels faster?   21.____

22.

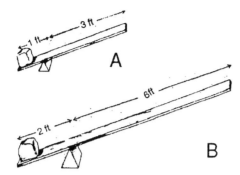

With which arrangement can a man lift the heavier weight?

22.____

23.

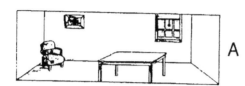

Which room has more of an echo?

23.____

24.

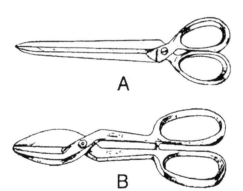

Which would be the BETTER shears for cutting metal?

24.____

KEY (CORRECT ANSWERS)

1.	A	11.	B
2.	A	12.	C
3.	A	13.	B
4.	A	14.	C
5.	B	15.	A
6.	A	16.	A
7.	B	17.	C
8.	B	18.	A
9.	A	19.	A
10.	A	20.	A

21.	B
22.	B
23.	A
24.	B

———

MECHANICAL APTITUDE

EXAMINATION SECTION
TEST 1

QUESTIONS 1-6.

Questions 1 through 6 are questions designed to test your ability to distinguish identical forms from unlike forms.

In each question, there are five drawings, lettered A, B, C, D, and E. Four of the drawings are alike. You are to find the one drawing that is different from the other four in the question. Then, on the Answer Sheet, blacken the space lettered the same as the figure that you have selected.

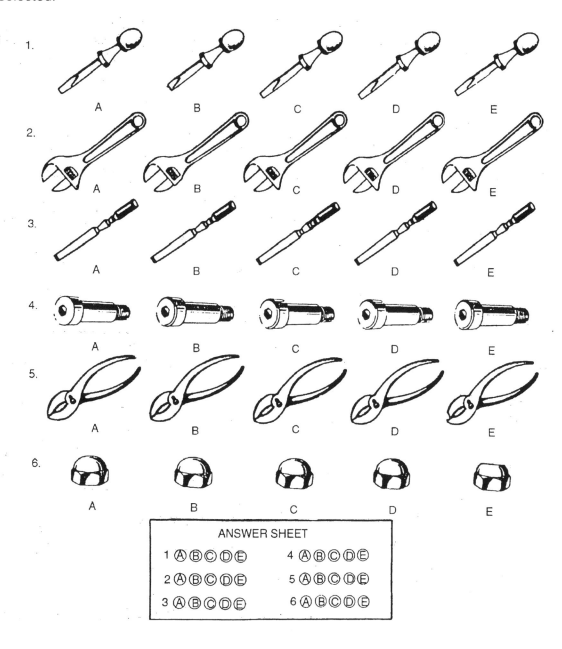

ANSWER SHEET

1 Ⓐ Ⓑ Ⓒ Ⓓ Ⓔ			4 Ⓐ Ⓑ Ⓒ Ⓓ Ⓔ	
2 Ⓐ Ⓑ Ⓒ Ⓓ Ⓔ			5 Ⓐ Ⓑ Ⓒ Ⓓ Ⓔ	
3 Ⓐ Ⓑ Ⓒ Ⓓ Ⓔ			6 Ⓐ Ⓑ Ⓒ Ⓓ Ⓔ	

QUESTIONS 7-8.

Questions 7 and 8 are questions designed to test your knowledge of pattern matching.

Questions 7 and 8 present problems found in making patterns. Each shows, at the left side, two or more separate flat pieces. In each question, select the arrangement lettered A, B, C, or D that shows how these pieces at the left can be fitted together without gaps or overlapping. The pieces may be turned around or turned over in any way to make them fit together.

On the Answer Sheet blacken the space lettered the same as the figure that you have selected.

Now, look at the questions below.

7.   From these pieces, which one of these arrangements can you make?

A   B   C   D

In question 7, only the arrangement D can be made from the pieces shown at the left, so space D is marked for Question 7 on the answer sheet below. (Note that it is necessary to turn the pieces around so that the short sides are at the bottom in the arrangement lettered D. None of the other arrangements show pieces of the given size and shape.)

8.   From these pieces, which one of these arrangements can you make?

A   B   C   D

ANSWER SHEET

7 Ⓐ Ⓑ Ⓒ Ⓓ

8 Ⓐ Ⓑ Ⓒ Ⓓ

QUESTIONS 9-10.

Questions 9 and 10. are questions designed to test your ability to identify forms of *LIKE* and *UNLIKE* proportions.

In each of the questions, select from the drawings of objects labeled A, B, C, and D, the one that would have the Top, Front, and Right views shown in the drawing at the left. Then on your Answer Sheet blacken the space that has the same letter as your answer.

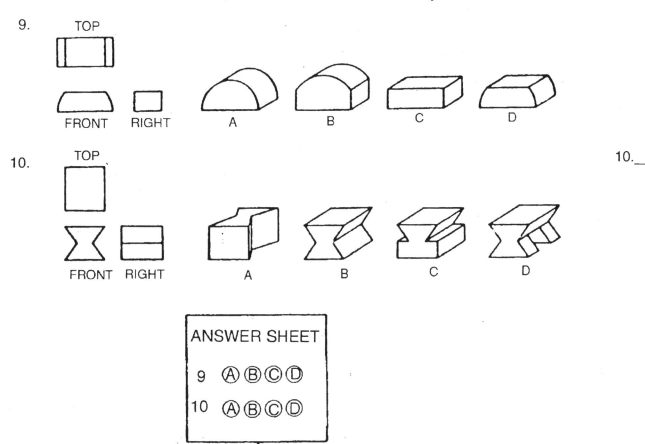

9.

TOP

FRONT   RIGHT   A   B   C   D

10.

TOP

10.____

FRONT   RIGHT   A   B   C   D

ANSWER SHEET

9   Ⓐ Ⓑ Ⓒ Ⓓ

10   Ⓐ Ⓑ Ⓒ Ⓓ

QUESTIONS 11-14.

Explanation and Commentary:

In each question, *ONE* rectangle is clearly *WRONG*. For each question, use the measuirng gage to check each of the rectangles and to find the *WRONG* one. Do this by putting the measuring gage rectangle on the question rectangle with the same letter so that the rectangles slightly overlap and the thin lines are parallel, like the one at the right. In this case, the height of the question rectangle exactly matches the height of the measuring gage rectangle, so the question rectangle is the right height. In this case, you do *NOT* mark your answer sheet.

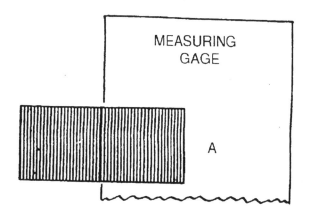

MEASURING GAGE

A

Once in every question, when you put a measuring gage rectangle on a question rectangle, you will find that the heights do *NOT* match and that the question rectangle is clearly wrong, like the one at the right. In this case, you mark on the answer sheet the space with the same letter as the wrong rectangle. *REMEMBER TO LINE UP THE MEASURING RECTANGLE WITH EACH QUESTION RECTANGLE SO THAT THE THIN LINES ARE EXACTLY PARALLEL.*

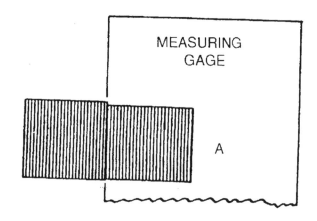

Now, cut out the measuring gage on the last page and practice on the questions. The test will be timed, so practice doing them rapidly and accurately.

Questions 11 through 14 test how quickly and accurately you can check the heights of rectangles with a measuring gage. Each question has five rectangles of different heights. The height is the dimension that runs the same way as the thin lines.

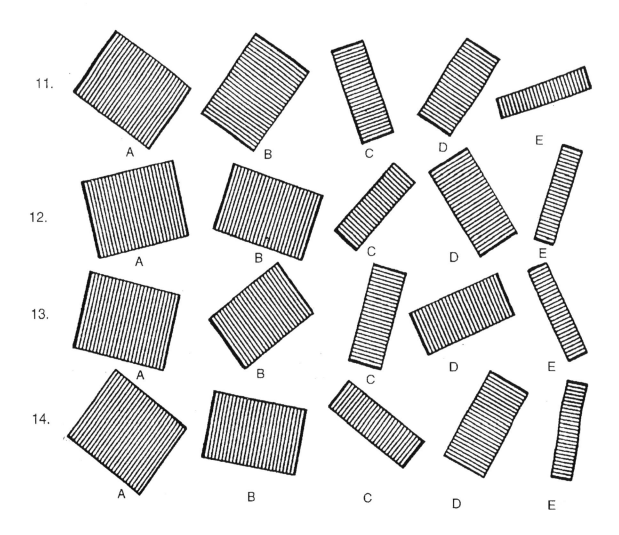

ANSWER SHEET

11 Ⓐ Ⓑ Ⓒ Ⓓ Ⓔ

12 Ⓐ Ⓑ Ⓒ Ⓓ Ⓔ

13 Ⓐ Ⓑ Ⓒ Ⓓ Ⓔ

14 Ⓐ Ⓑ Ⓒ Ⓓ Ⓔ

MEASURING
GAGE

 A

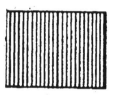 B

 C

 D

 E

KEY (CORRECT ANSWERS)

1.	B		8.	B
2.	B		9.	D
3.	C		10.	B
4.	A		11.	D
5.	E		12.	C
6.	E		13.	B
7.	D		14.	A

MECHANICAL APTITUDE

EXAMINATION SECTION
TEST 1

MECHANICAL COMPREHENSION

DIRECTIONS: Questions 1 to 4 test your ability to understand general mechanical devices. Pictures are shown and questions asked about the mechanical devices shown in the picture. Read each question and study the picture. Each question is followed by four choices. For each question, choose the one BEST answer (A, B, C, or D). Then *PRINT THE LETTER OF THE CORRECT ANSWER IN THE SPACE AT THE RIGHT.*

1. The reason for crossing the belt connecting these wheels is to   1.____

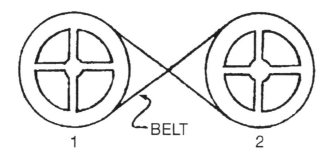

   A. make the wheels turn in opposite directions
   B. make wheel 2 turn faster than wheel 1
   C. save wear on the belt
   D. take up slack in the belt

2. The purpose of the small gear between the two large gears is to   2.____

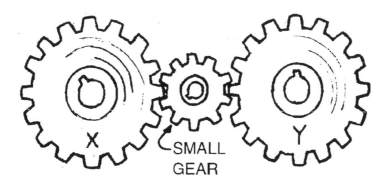

   A. increase the speed of the larger gears
   B. allow the larger gears to turn in different directions
   C. decrease the speed of the larger gears
   D. make the larger gears turn in the same direction

3. Each of these three-foot-high water cans have a bottom with an area of-one square foot.   3._____
    The pressure on the bottom of the cans is

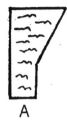 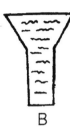 

A   B   C

A. least in A   B. least in B
C. least in C   D. the same in all

4. The reading on the scale should be   4._____

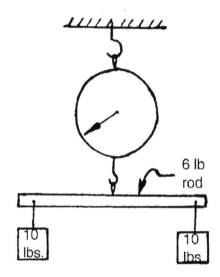

6 lb
rod

A. zero
B. 10 pounds
C. 13 pounds
D. 26 pounds

———

KEY (CORRECT ANSWERS)

1. A
2. D
3. D
4. D

———

TEST 2

DIRECTIONS: Questions 1 to 6 test knowledge of tools and how to use them. For each question, decide which one of the four things shown in the boxes labeled A, B, C, or D normally is used with or goes best with the thing in the picture on the left. Then *PRINT THE LETTER OF THE CORRECT ANSWER IN THE SPACE AT THE RIGHT.*

NOTE: All tools are NOT drawn to the same scale.

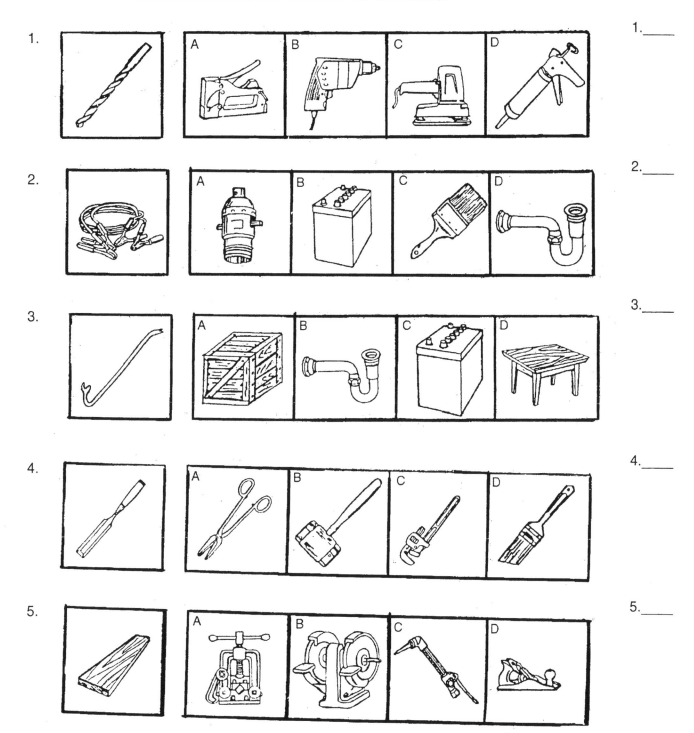

1. _____

2. _____

3. _____

4. _____

5. _____

6.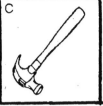

6.____

———

KEY (CORRECT ANSWERS)

1. B   4. B
2. B   5. D
3. A   6. B

———

MECHANICAL APTITUDE
MECHANICAL COMPREHENSION
EXAMINATION SECTION
TEST 1

DIRECTIONS : Each question or incomplete statement below is followed by several suggested answers or completions. Select the *one* that *BEST* answers the question or completes the statement. *PRINT THE LETTER OF THE CORRECT ANSWER IN THE SPACE AT THE RIGHT.*

Questions 1-3.

DIRECTIONS: Questions 1 to 3 inclusive are based upon the following paragraph.

The only openings permitted in fire partitions except openings for ventilating ducts shall be those required for doors. There shall be but one such door opening unless the provision of additional openings would not exceed, in total width of all doorways, 25 percent of the length of the wall. The minimum distance between openings shall be three feet. The maximum area for such a door opening shall be 80 square feet, except that such openings for the passage of motor trucks may be a maximum of 140 square feet.

1. According to the above paragraph, openings in fire partitions are permitted *only* for   1____

    A. doors
    B. doors and windows
    C. doors and ventilation ducts
    D. doors, windows and ventilation ducts

2. In a fire partition, 22 feet long and 10 feet high, the *MAXIMUM* number of doors, 3 feet   2____
    wide and 7 feet high, is

    A. 1   B. 2   C. 3   D. 4

3.   3____

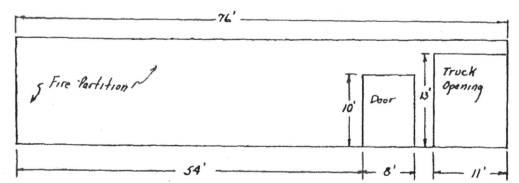

The **one** of the following statements about the layout shown above that is *MOST* accurate is that the

    A. total width of the openings is too large
    B. truck opening is too large
    C. truck and door openings are too close together
    D. layout is acceptable

4. At a given temperature, a wet hand will freeze to a bar of metal, but *NOT* to a piece of wood, because the   4____

     A. metal expands and contracts more than the wood
     B. wood is softer than the metal
     C. wood will burn at a lower temperature than the metal
     D. metal is a better conductor of heat than the wood

5. Of the following items commonly found in a household, the one that uses the *MOST* electric current is a(n)   5____

     A. 150-watt light bulb   B. toaster
     C. door buzzer   D. 8" electric fan

6. Sand and ashes are frequently placed on icy pavements to prevent skidding. The effect of the sand and ashes is to increase   6____

     A. inertia   B. gravity   C. momentum   D. friction

7. The air near the ceiling of a room usually is warmer than the air near the floor because   7____

     A. there is better air circulation at the floor level
     B. warm air is lighter than cold air
     C. windows usually are nearer the floor than the ceiling
     D. heating pipes usually run along the ceiling

8.   8____

Dia. 1   *Dia. 2*

It is safer to use the ladder positioned as shown in diagram 1 than as shown in diagram 2 because, in diagram 1,

     A. less strain is placed upon the center rungs of the ladder
     B. it is easier to grip and stand on the ladder
     C. the ladder reaches a lower height
     D. the ladder is less likely to tip over backwards

9.

9_____

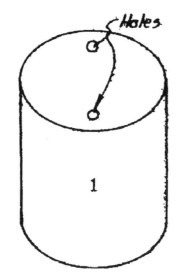

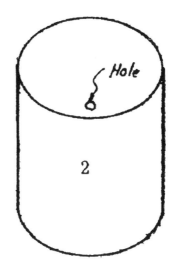

It is *easier* to pour a liquid from:

A. Can 1 because there are two holes from which the liquid can flow
B. Can 1 because air can enter through one hole while the liquid comes out the other hole
C. Can 2 because the liquid comes out under greater pressure
D. Can 2 because it is easier to direct the flow of the liquid when there is only one hole

10. A substance which is subject to "spontaneous combustion" is one that

10_____

A. is explosive when heated
B. is capable of catching fire without an external source of heat
C. acts to speed up the burning of material
D. liberates oxygen when heated

11. The sudden shutting down of a nozzle on a hose discharging water under high pressure is a *bad* practice CHIEFLY because the

11_____

A. hose is likely to whip about violently
B. hose is likely to burst
C. valve handle is likely to snap
D. valve handle is likely to jam

12. Fire can continue where there are present fuel, oxygen from the air or other source, and a sufficiently high temperature to maintain combustion. The method of extinguishment of fire MOST commonly used is to

12_____

A. remove the fuel
B. exclude the oxygen from the burning material
C. reduce the temperature of the burning material
D. smother the flames of the burning material

13.

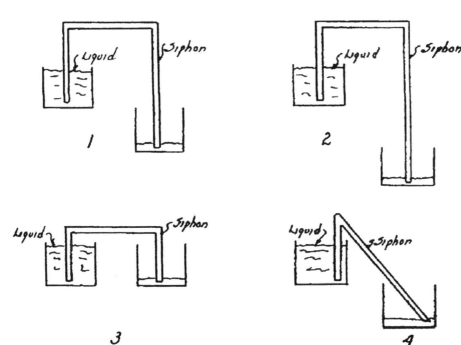

The *one* of the siphon arrangements shown above which would *MOST* quickly transfer a solution from the container on the left side to the one on the right side is numbered

A. 1   B. 2   C. 3   D. 4

14. Static electricity is a hazard in industry CHIEFLY because it may cause

A. dangerous or painful burns
B. chemical decomposition of toxic elements
C. sparks which can start an explosion
D. overheating of electrical equipment

15.

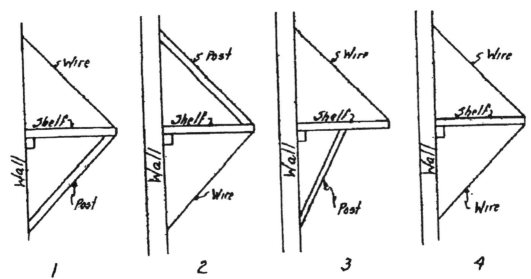

The *STRONGEST* method of supporting the shelf is shown in diagram

A. 1   B. 2   C. 3   D. 4

16. A row boat will float *deeper* in fresh water than in salt water *because* 16____

    A. in the salt water the salt will occupy part of the space
    B. fresh water is heavier than salt water
    C. salt water is heavier than fresh water
    D. salt water offers less resistance than fresh water

17. 17____

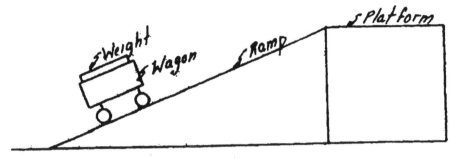

It is easier to get the load onto the platform by using the ramp than it is to lift it directly onto the platform. This is *true* because the effect of the ramp is to

    A. reduce the amount of friction so that less force is required
    B. distribute the weight over a larger area
    C. support part of the load so that less force is needed to move the wagon
    D. increase the effect of the moving weight

18. 18____

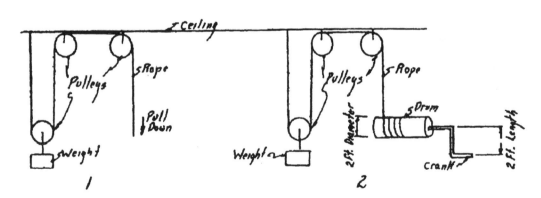

More weight can be lifted by the method shown in diagram 2 than as shown in diagram 1 because

    A. it takes less force to turn a crank than it does to pull in a straight line
    B. the drum will prevent the weight from falling by itself
    C. the length of the crank is larger than the radius of the drum
    D. the drum has more rope on it easing the pull

19.   19____

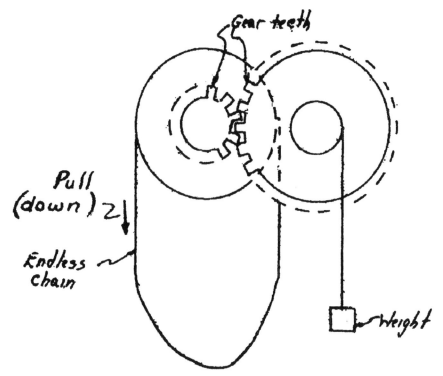

As the endless chain is pulled down in the direction shown, the weight will move

    A.   *up* faster than the endless chain is pulled down
    B.   *up* slower than the endless chain is pulled down
    C.   *down* faster than the endless chain is pulled down
    D.   *down* slower than the endless chain is pulled down

20. Two balls of the same size, but different weights, are both dropped from a 10-ft. height.   20____
    The one of the following statements that is *MOST* accurate is that

    A.   both balls will reach the ground at the same time because they are the same size
    B.   both balls will reach the ground at the same time because the effect of gravity is
         the same on both balls
    C.   the heavier ball will reach the ground first because it weighs more
    D.   the lighter ball will reach the ground first because air resistance is greater on the
         heavier ball

21. It is considered poor practice to increase the leverage of a wrench by placing a pipe over   21____
    the handle of the wrench. This is true *PRINCIPALLY* because

    A.   the wrench may break
    B.   the wrench may slip off the nut
    C.   it is harder to place the wrench on the nut
    D.   the wrench is more difficult to handle

22.

22____

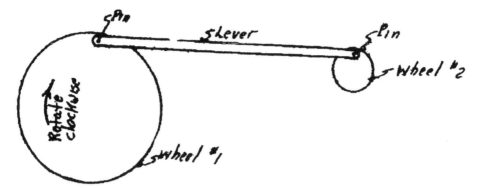

If wheel #1 is turned in the direction shown, wheel #2 will

- A. turn continously in a clockwise direction
- B. turn continously in a counterclockwise direction
- C. move back and fourth
- D. became jammed and both wheels will shop

23. ALL SOLID AREAS REPRESENT EQUAL WEIGHTS ATTACHED TO THE FLYWHEEL   23____

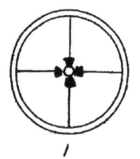 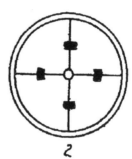 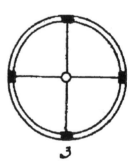

The above diagrams are of flywheels made of the same material with the same dimensions and attached to similar engines. The solid areas represent equal weights attached to the fly wheel. If all three engines are running at the same speed for the same length of time and the power to the engines is shut of simultaneously,

- A. wheel 1 will continue turning longest
- B. wheel 2 will continue turning longest
- C. wheel 3 will continue turning longest
- D. all three wheels will continue turning for the same time

24. The one of the following substance which expands when freezing is   24____

    A. alcohol   B. ammonia   C. mercury   D. water

25. A piece of copper wire 30 feet long is cut into two pieces, 20 feet and 10 feet. The resistance of the *longer* piece, compared to the shorter, is   25____

- A. one-half as much
- B. two-thirds as much
- C. one and one-half as much
- D. twice as much

KEY (CORRECT ANSWERS)

1. C	11. B
2. A	12. C
3. B	13. B
4. D	14. C
5. B	15. A
6. D	16. C
7. B	17. C
8. D	18. C
9. B	19. D
10. B	20. B

21. A
22. D
23. C
24. D
25. D

TEST 2

DIRECTIONS: Each question or incomplete statement below is followed by several suggested answers or completions. Select the *one* that *BEST* answers the question or completes the statement. *PRINT THE LETTER OF THE CORRECT ANSWER IN THE SPACE AT THE RIGHT.*

Questions 1-2.

DIRECTIONS: Questions 1 and 2 are to be answered in accordance with the information in the following statement:

The electrical resistance of copper wires varies directly with their lengths and inversely with their cross section areas.

1. A piece of copper wire 30 feet long is cut into two pieces, 20 feet and 10 feet. The resistance of the *longer* piece, compared to the shorter, is

    A. one-half as much
    B. two-thirds as much
    C. one and one-half as much
    D. twice as much

1___

2. Two pieces of copper wire are each 10 feet long but the cross section area of one is 2/3 that of the other. The resistance of the piece with the *larger* cross-section area is

    A. one-half the resistance of the smaller
    B. two-thirds the resistance of the smaller
    C. one and one-half times the resistance of the smaller
    D. twice the resistance of the smaller

2___

3.

3___

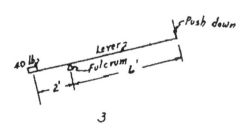

The arrangement of the lever which would require the *LEAST* amount of force to move the weight is shown in the diagram numbered

    A. 1   B. 2   C. 3   D. 4

4. Steel supporting beams in buildings often are surrounded by a thin layer of concrete to keep the beams from becoming hot and collapsing during a fire.
The *one* of the following statements which *BEST* explains how collapse is prevented by this arrangement is that concrete

4___

    A. becomes stronger as its temperature is increased

B. acts as an insulating material
C. protects the beam from rust and corrosion
D. reacts chemically with steel at high temperatures

5. If boiling water is poured into a drinking glass, the glass is likely to crack. If, however, a metal spoon first is placed in the glass, it is much less likely to crack. The reason that the glass with the spoon is *less likely* to crack is that the spoon

  A. distributes the water over a larger surface of the glass
  B. quickly absorbs heat from the water
  C. reinforces the glass
  D. reduces the amount of water which can be poured into the glass

6. It takes *more* energy to force water through a *long* pipe than through a *short* pipe of the same diameter. The PRINCIPAL reason for this is

  A. gravity   B. friction   C. inertia   D. cohesion

7. A pump, discharging at 300 lbs.-per-sq.-inch pressure, delivers water through 100 feet of pipe laid horizontally. If the valve at the end of the pipe is shut so that no water can flow, then the pressure at the valve is, for practical purposes,

  A. *greater* than the pressure at the pump
  B. *equal to* the pressure at the pump
  C. *less* than the pressure at the pump
  D. *greater or less* than the pressure at the pump, depending on the type of pump used

8. The explosive force of a gas when stored under various pressures is given in the following table:

Storage Pressure	Explosive Force
10	1
20	8
30	27
40	64
50	125

The *one* of the following statements which BEST expresses the relationship between the storage pressure and explosive force is that
  A. there is no systematic relationship between an increase in storage pressure and an increase in explosive force
  B. the explosive force varies as the square of the pressure
  C. the explosive force varies as the cube of the pressure
  D. the explosive force varies as the fourth power of the pressure

9.

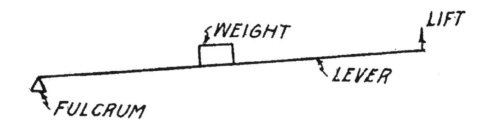

The leverage system in the sketch above is used to raise a weight. In order to *reduce* the amount of force required to raise the weight, it is necessary to

A. decrease the length of the lever
B. place the weight closer to the fulcrum
C. move the weight closer to the person applying the force
D. move the fulcrum further from the weight

10. In the accompanying sketch of a block and fall, if the end of the rope P is pulled so that it moves one foot, the distance the weight will be *raised* is

A. 1/2 ft.
B. 1 ft.
C. 1 1/2 ft.
D. 2 ft.

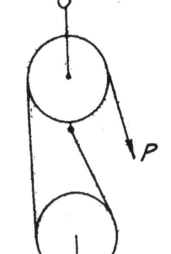

11.   11_____

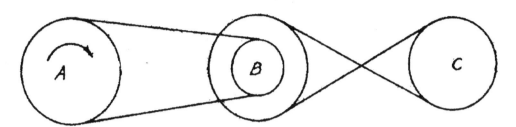

The above sketch diagrammatically shows a pulley and belt system. If pulley A is made to rotate in a clockwise direction, *then* pulley C will rotate

A. faster than pulley A and in a clockwise direction
B. slower than pulley A and in a clockwise direction
C. faster than pulley A and in a counter-clockwise direction
D. slower than pulley A and in a counter-clockwise direction

12.   12_____

  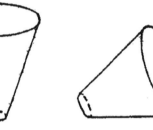 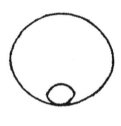

The above diagrams show four positions of the same object. The position in which this object is *MOST* stable is

A. 1   B. 2   C. 3   D. 4

13. The accompanying sketch dia-   13_____
grammatically shows a system of
meshing gears with relative diameters as drawn. If gear 1 is made
to rotate in the direction of the
arrow, *then* the gear that will turn
FASTEST is numbered

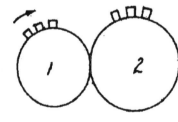

A. 1   B. 2   C. 3   D. 4

14.   14_____

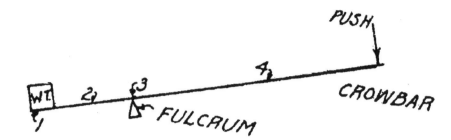

The above sketch shows a weight being lifted by means of a crowbar.
The point at which the tendency for the bar to break is GREATEST is

A. 1   B. 2   C. 3   D. 4

15.   15_____

The above sketches show four objects which weigh the same but have different shapes.
The object which is MOST difficult to tip over is numbered

A. 1   B. 2   C. 3   D. 4

16.   16_____

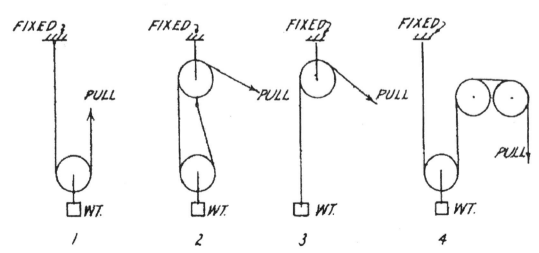

An object is to be lifted by means of a system of lines and pulleys. Of the systems shown above, the one which would require the GREATEST force to be used in lifting the weight is the one numbered

A. 1   B. 2   C. 3   D. 4

17. An intense fire develops in a room in which carbon dioxide cylinders are stored. The
PRINCIPAL hazard in this situation is that

  17_____

  A. the CO_2 may catch fire
  B. toxic fumes may be released
  C. the cylinders may explode
  D. released CO_2 may intensify the fire

18. At a fire involving the roof of a 5-story building, the firemen trained their hose stream on
the fire from a vacant lot across the street, aiming the stream at a point about 15 feet
above the roof.
In this situation, water in the stream would be traveling at the GREATEST speed

  18_____

  A. as it leaves the hose nozzle
  B. at a point midway between the ground and the roof
  C. at the maximum height of the stream
  D. as it drops on the roof

19. A principle of lighting is that the intensity of illumination at a point is inversely proportional
to the square of the distance from the source of illumination.
Assume that a pulley lamp is lowered from a position of 6 feet to one of three feet
above a desk. According to the above principle, we would expect that the amount of
illumination reaching the desk from the lamp in the lower position, as compared to the
higher position, will be

  19_____

  A. half as much   B. twice as much
  C. four times as much   D. nine times as much

20.

  20_____

  1   2   3   4

When standpipes are required in a structure, sufficient risers must be installed so that
no point on the floor is more than 120 feet from a riser.
The one of the above diagrams which gives the MAXIMUM area which can be covered
by one riser is

  A. 1   B. 2   C. 3   D. 4

21. Spontaneous combustion may be the reason for a pile of oily rags catching fire.
In general, spontaneous combustion is the DIRECT result of

  21_____

  A. application of flame   B. falling sparks
  C. intense sunlight   D. chemical action
  E. radioactivity

22. In general, firemen are advised not to direct a solid stream of water on fires burning in   22____
    electrical equipment. Of the following, the *MOST* logical reason for this instruction is that

    A. water is a conductor of electricity
    B. water will do more damage to the electrical equipment than the fire
    C. hydrogen in water may explode when it comes in contact with electric current
    D. water will not effectively extinguish fires in electrical equipment
    E. water may spread the fire to other circuits

23. The height at which a fireboat will float in still water is determined *CHIEFLY* by the   23____

    A. weight of the water displaced by the boat

    B. horsepower of the boat's engines

    C. number of propellers on the boat

    D. curve the bow has above the water line

    E. skill with which the boat is maneuvered

24. When firemen are working at the nozzle of a hose they usually lean forward on the hose.   24____
    The *most likely* reason for taking this position is that

    A. the surrounding air is cooled, making the firemen more comfortable
    B. a backward force is developed which must be counteracted
    C. the firemen can better see where the stream strikes
    D. the fireman are better protected from injury by falling debris
    E. the stream is projected further

25. In general, the color and odor of smoke will *BEST* indicate   25____

    A. the cause of the fire
    B. the extent of the fire
    C. how long the fire has been burning
    D. the kind of material on fire
    E. the exact seat of the fire

KEY (CORRECT ANSWERS)

1.	D	11.	C
2.	B	12.	A
3.	A	13.	D
4.	B	14.	C
5.	B	15.	A
6.	B	16.	C
7.	B	17.	C
8.	C	18.	A
9.	B	19.	C
10.	A	20.	C

21. D
22. A
23. A
24. B
25. D

———————

TEST 3

DIRECTIONS : Each question or incomplete statement below is followed by several suggested answers or completions. Select the *one* that *BEST* answers the question or completes the statement. *PRINT THE LETTER OF THE CORRECT ANSWER IN THE SPACE AT THE RIGHT.*

1. As a demonstration, firemen set up two hose lines identical in every respect except that one was longer than the other. Water was then delivered through these lines from one pump and it was seen that the stream from the longer hose line had a shorter "throw," Of the following, the *MOST* valid explanation of this difference in "throw" is that the   1____

    A. air resistance to the water stream is proportional to the length of hose
    B. time required for water to travel through the longer hose is greater than for the shorter one
    C. loss due to friction is greater in the longer hose than in the shorter one
    D. rise of temperature is greater in the longer hose than in the shorter one
    E. longer hose line probably developed a leak at one of the coupling joints

2. Of the following toxic gases, the *one* which is *MOST* dangerous because it cannot be seen and has no odor, is   2____

    A. ether   B. carbon monoxide   C. chlorine
    D. ammonia   E. cooking gas

3. You are visiting with some friends when their young son rushes into the room with his clothes on fire. You immediately wrap him in a rug and roll him on the floor. The *MOST* important reason for your action is that the   3____

    A. flames are confined within the rug
    B. air supply to the fire is reduced
    C. burns sustained will be third degree, rather than first degree
    D. whirling action will put out the fire
    E. boy will not suffer from shock

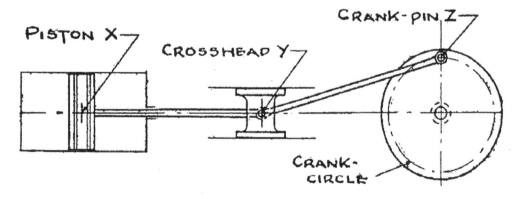

FIGURE I

Questions 4-6,

DIRECTIONS: The device shown in Figure I above represents schematically a mechanism
                commonly used to change reciprocating (back and forth) motion to rotation
                (circular) motion.
The following questions, numbered 4 to 6 inclusive, are to be answered with reference to
this device.

4.   Assume that piston X is placed in its extreme left position so that X, Y and Z are in a hor-   4____
     izontal line. If a horizontal force to the right is applied to the piston X, we may then expect
     that

     A.   the crank-pin Z will revolve clockwise
     B.   the crosshead Y will move in a direction opposite to that of X
     C.   the crank-pin Z will revolve counterclockwise
     D.   no movement will take place
     E.   the crank-pin Z will oscillate back and forth

5.   If we start from the position shown in the above diagram, and move piston X to the right,   5____
     the result will be that

     A.   the crank-pin Z will revolve counterclockwise and cross-head Y will move to the left
     B.   the crank-pin Z will revolve clockwise and crosshead Y will move to the left
     C.   the crank-pin Z will revolve clockwise and crosshead Y will move to the right
     D.   the crank-pin Z will revolve clockwise and crosshead Y will move to the right
     E.   crosshead Y will move to the left as piston X moves to the right

6.   If crank-pin Z is moved closer to the center of the crank circle, then the length of the   6____

     A.   stroke of piston X is increased
     B.   stroke of piston X is decreased
     C.   stroke of piston X is unchanged
     D.   rod between the piston X and crosshead Y is increased
     E.   rod between the piston X and crosshead Y is decreased

Questions 7-8.

DIRECTIONS: Figure II represents schematically a block-and-fall tackle. The advantage
                derived from this machine is that the effect of the applied force is multiplied by
                the number of lines of rope directly supporting the load. The following two
                questions, numbered 7 and 8, are to be answered with reference to this figure.

7.   Pull P is exerted on line T to raise the load L. The line in which the *LARGEST* strain is   7____
     finally induced is line

     A. T   B. U   C. V   D. X   E. Y

8. If the largest pull P that two men can apply to line T is 280 lbs., the *MAXIMUM* load L that they can raise without regard to frictional losses is, *most nearly,* _____ lbs.
   A. 1960
   B. 1680
   C. 1400
   D. 1260
   E. 1120

8 _____

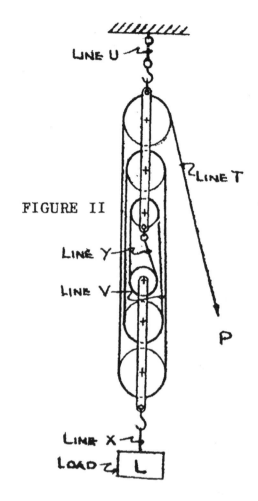

FIGURE II

Questions 9-13.

DIRECTIONS: Answer Questions 9 to 13 on the basis of Figure III. The diagram schematically illustrates part of a water tank. 1 and 5 are outlet and inlet pipes, respectively. 2 is a valve which can be used to open and close the outlet pipe by hand. 3 is a float which is rigidly connected to valve 4 by an iron bar, thus causing that valve to open or shut as the float rises or falls 4 is a hinged valve which controls the flow of water into the tank.

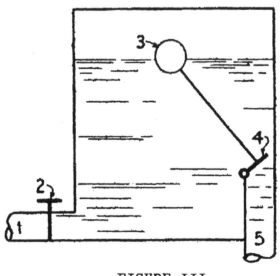

FIGURE III

9. If the tank is half filled and water is going out of pipe 1 more rapidly than it is coming in   9___
through pipe 5, *then*

    A. valve 2 is closed   B. float 3 is rising in the tank
    C. valve 4 is opening wider   D. valve 4 is closed
    E. float 3 is stationary

10. If the tank is half filled with water and water is coming in through inlet pipe 5 more rapidly   10___
than it is going out through outlet pipe 1, *then*

    A. valve 2 is closed   B. float 3 is rising in the tank
    C. valve 4 is opening wider   D. valve 4 is closed
    E. float 3 is stationary

11. If the tank is empty, then it can *normally* be expected that   11___

    A. float 3 is at its highest position
    B. float 3 is at its lowest position
    C. valve 2 is closed
    D. valve 4 is closed
    E. water will not come into the tank

12. If float 3 develops a leak, *then*   12___

    A. the tank will tend to empty
    B. water will tend to stop coming into the tank
    C. valve 4 will tend to close
    D. valve 2 will tend to close
    E. valve 4 will tend to remain open

13. Without any other changes being made, if the bar joining the float to valve 4 is removed   13___
and a slightly shorter bar substituted, *then*

    A. a smaller quantity of water in the tank will be required before the float closes valve
        4
    B. valve 4 will not open
    C. valve 4 will not close
    D. it is not possible to determine what will happen
    E. a greater quantity of water in the tank will be required before the float closes
        valve 4

Questions 14-18.

DIRECTIONS: Answer Questions 14 to 18 on the basis of Figure IV. A, B, C and D are four
meshed gears forming a gear train. Gear A is the driver. Gears A and D each
have twice as many teeth as gear B, and gear C has four times as many teeth
as gear B. The diagram is schematic: the teeth go all around each gear.

14. *Two* gears which turn in the *same* direction are: 14___

    A. A and B   B. B and C   C. C and D
    D. D and A   E. B and D

15. The *two* gears which
revolve at the *same* speed
are gears

15____

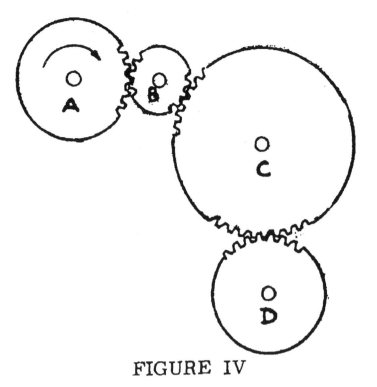

FIGURE IV

A. A and C   B. A and D   C. B and C
D. B and D   E. D and C

16. If all the teeth on gear C are stripped without affecting the teeth on gears A, B, and D,   16____
then rotation would occur *only* in gear(s)

A. C   B. D   C. A and B
D. A, B, and D   E. B and D

17. If gear D is rotating at the rate of 100 RPM, then gear B is rotating at the rate of _____   17____
RPM.

A. 25   B. 50   C. 100   D. 200   E. 400

18. If gear A turns at the rate of two revolutions per second, then the number of revolutions   18____
per second that gear C turns is

A. 1   B. 2   C. 3   D. 4   E. 8

Questions 19-23.

DIRECTIONS: Answer Questions 19 to 23 on the basis of Figure V. The diagram shows a water pump in cross section: 1 is a check valve, 2 and 3 are the spring and diaphragm, respectively, of the discharge valve, 4 is the pump piston; 5 is the inlet valve, and 6 is the pump cylinder. All valves permit the flow of water in one direction only.

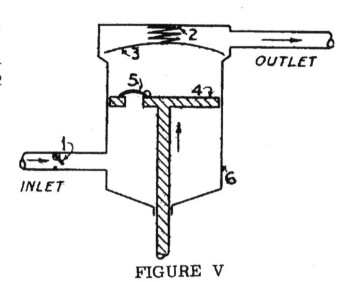

FIGURE V

19.   When water is flowing through the outlet pipe,   19____

    A.   check valve 1 is closed   B.   diaphragm 3 is closed
    C.   valve 5 is closed   D.   spring 2 is fully extended
    E.   the piston is on the downstroke

20.   If valve 5 does not work properly and stays closed, *then*   20____

    A.   the piston cannot move down   B.   the piston cannot move up
    C.   diaphragm 3 cannot open   D.   check valve 1 cannot close
    E.   the flow of water will be reversed

21.   If diaphragm 3 does not work properly and stays in the open position, *then*   21____

    A.   check valve 1 will not open
    B.   valve 5 will not open
    C.   spring 2 will be compressed
    D.   spring 2 will be extended
    E.   water will not flow through the inlet pipe

22.   When valve 5 is open during normal operation of the pump, *then*   22____

    A.   spring 2 is fully compressed
    B.   the piston is on the upstroke
    C.   water is flowing through check valve 1
    D.   a vacuum is formed between the piston and the bottom of the cylinder
    E.   diaphragm 3 is closed

23.   If check valve 1 jams and stays closed, *then*   23____

    A.   valve 5 will be open on both the upstroke and down stroke of the piston
    B.   a vacuum will tend to form in the inlet pipe between the source of the water supply and check valve 1
    C.   pressure on the cylinder side of check valve 1 will increase

D. less force will be required to move the piston down
E. more force will be required to move the piston down

24. The one of the following which *BEST* explains why smoke usually rises from a fire is that   24____

A. cooler, heavier air displaces lighter, warm air
B. heat energy of the fire propels the smoke upward
C. suction from the upper air pulls the smoke upward
D. burning matter is chemically changed into heat energy

25. The practice of racing a car engine to warm it up in cold weather, generally, is   25____

A. *good, MAINLY* because repeated stalling of the engine and drain on the battery is avoided
B. *bad, MAINLY* because too much gas is used to get the engine heated
C. *good, MAINLY* because the engine becomes operational in the shortest period of time
D. *bad, MAINLY* because proper lubrication is not established rapidly enough

————————

KEY (CORRECT ANSWERS)

1.	C		11.	B
2.	B		12.	E
3.	B		13.	A
4.	D		14.	E
5.	D		15.	B
6.	B		16.	C
7.	B		17.	D
8.	B		18.	A
9.	C		19.	C
10.	B		20.	A

21.	C
22.	E
23.	D
24.	A
25.	D

————————

READING COMPREHENSION
UNDERSTANDING AND INTERPRETING WRITTEN MATERIAL
EXAMINATION SECTION
TEST 1

DIRECTIONS: Each question or incomplete statement is followed by-several suggested answers or completions. Select the one that BEST answers the question or completes the statement. *PRINT THE LETTER OF THE CORRECT ANSWER IN THE SPACE AT THE RIGHT.*

Questions 1-3.

DIRECTIONS: Questions 1 through 3, inclusive, are to be answered in accordance with the following paragraph.

All cement work contracts, more or less, in setting. The contraction in concrete walls and other structures causes fine cracks to develop at regular intervals. The tendency to contract increases in direct proportion to the quantity of cement in the concrete. A rich mixture will contract more than a lean mixture. A concrete wall which has been made of a very lean mixture and which has been built by filling only about one foot in depth of concrete in the form each day will frequently require close inspection to reveal the cracks.

1. According to the above paragraph,   1.____

    A.   shrinkage seldom occurs in concrete
    B.   shrinkage occurs only in certain types of concrete
    C.   by placing concrete at regular intervals, shrinkage may be avoided
    D.   it is impossible to prevent shrinkage

2. According to the above paragraph, the one of the factors which reduces shrinkage in   2.____
concrete is the

    A.   volume of concrete in wall
    B.   height of each day's pour
    C.   length of wall
    D.   length and height of wall

3. According to the above paragraph, a rich mixture   3.____

    A.   pours the easiest
    B.   shows the largest amount of cracks
    C.   is low in cement content
    D.   need not be inspected since cracks are few

Questions 4-6.

DIRECTIONS: Questions 4 through 6, inclusive, are to be answered SOLELY on the basis of the following paragraph.

It is best to avoid surface water on freshly poured concrete in the first place. However, when there is a very small amount present, the recommended procedure is to allow it to evaporate before finishing. If there is considerable water, it is removed with a broom, belt, float, or by other convenient means. It is never good practice to sprinkle dry cement, or a mixture of cement and fine aggregate, on concrete to take up surface water. Such fine materials form a layer on the surface that is likely to dust or hair check when the concrete hardens.

4. The MAIN subject of the above passage is 4._____

    A. surface cracking of concrete
    B. evaporation of water from freshly poured concrete
    C. removing surface water from concrete
    D. final adjustments of ingredients in the concrete mix

5. According to the above passage, the sprinkling of dry cement on the surface of a concrete mix would MOST LIKELY 5._____

    A. prevent the mix from setting
    B. cause discoloration on the surface of the concrete
    C. cause the coarse aggregate to settle out too quickly
    D. cause powdering and small cracks on the surface of the concrete

6. According to the above passage, the thing to do when considerable surface water is present on the freshly poured concrete is to 6._____

    A. dump the concrete back into the mixer and drain the water
    B. allow the water to evaporate before finishing
    C. remove the water with a broom, belt, or float
    D. add more fine aggregate but not cement

Questions 7-9.

DIRECTIONS: Questions 7 through 9, inclusive, are to be answered ONLY in accordance with the information given in the paragraph below.

Before placing the concrete, check that the forms are rigid and well braced and place the concrete within 45 minutes after mixing it. Fill the forms to the top with the wearing-course concrete. Level off the surfaces with a strieboard. When the concrete becomes stiff but still workable (in a few hours), finish the surface with a wood float. This fills the hollows and compacts the concrete and produces a smooth but gritty finish. For a non-gritty and smoother surface (but one that is more slippery when wet), follow up with a steel trowel after the water sheen from the wood-troweling starts to disappear. If you wish, slant the tread forward a fraction of an inch so that it will shed rain water.

7. Slanting the tread a fraction of an inch gives a surface that will 7._____

    A. have added strength
    B. not be slippery when wet
    C. shed rain water
    D. not have hollows

8. In addition to giving a smooth but gritty finish, the use of a wood float will tend to   8.____

    A. give a finish that is slippery when wet
    B. compact the concrete
    C. give a better wearing course
    D. provide hollows to retain rain water

9. Which one of the following statements is most nearly correct?   9.____

    A. Having checked the forms, one may place the concrete immediately after mixing same.
    B. One must wait at least 15 minutes after mixing the concrete before it may be placed in the forms.
    C. A gritty compact finish and one which is more slippery when wet will result with the use of a wood float.
    D. A steel trowel used promptly after a wood float will tend to give a non-gritty smooth finish.

Questions 10-11.

DIRECTIONS: Questions 10 and 11 are to be answered SOLELY on the basis of information contained in the following paragraph.

Tools and plastering methods have changed very little over the years. Most of the changes are mere improvements of the basic tools. The tools formerly made by hand are now machine-made and are *rigidly* constructed of light, but strong, materials in contrast to the clumsy constructions of the early types. The power-driven mixers and hoisting equipment used on large plastering jobs today produce better mortars and lighten the tasks involved.

10. According to the above paragraph, present day tools used for plastering   10.____

    A. have made plastering much more complicated than it used to be
    B. are heavier than the old-fashioned tools they replaced
    C. produce poorer results but speed up the job
    D. are lighter and stronger than the hand-made tools of the past

11. As used in the above paragraph, the word *rigidly* means MOST NEARLY   11.____

    A. feeble   B. weakly   C. firmly   D. flexibly

Questions 12-18.

DIRECTIONS: Questions 12 through 18 are to be answered in accordance with the following paragraphs.

SURFACE RENEWING OVERLAYS

A surface renewing overlay should consist of material which can be constructed in very thin layers. The material must fill surface voids and provide an impervious skid-resistant surface. It must also be sufficiently resistant to traffic abrasion to provide an economical service life.

Materials meeting these requirements are:
      a. Asphalt concrete having small particle size
      b. Hot sand asphalts
      c. Surface seal coats

Fine-graded asphalt concrete or hot sand asphalt can be constructed in layers as thin as one-half inch and fulfill all requirements for surface renewing overlays. They are recommended for thin resurfacing of pavements having high traffic volumes, as their service lives are relatively long when constructed properly. They can be used for minor leveling, they are quiet riding, and their appearance is exceptionally pleasing. Seal coats or slurry seals may fulfill surface requirements for low traffic pavements.

12. A surface renewing overlay must fill surface voids, provide an impervious skid-resistant surface, and   12.____

    A. be resistant to traffic abrasion
    B. have small particle size
    C. be exceptionally pleasing in appearance
    D. be constructed in half-inch layers

13. An *impervious skid-resistant surface* means a surface that is   13.____

    A. rough to the touch and fixed firmly in place
    B. waterproof and provides good gripping for tires
    C. not damaged by skidding vehicles
    D. smooth to the touch and quiet riding

14. The number of types of materials that can be constructed in very thin layers and are also suitable for surface renewing overlays is   14.____

    A. 1   B. 2   C. 3   D. 4

15. The SMALLEST thickness of asphalt concrete or hot sand asphalt that can fulfill all requirements for surface renewing overlays is _____ inch(es).   15.____

    A. ¼   B. ½   C. 1   D. 2

16. The materials that are recommended for thin resurfacing of pavements having high traffic volumes are   16.____

    A. those that have relatively long service lives
    B. asphalt concretes with maximum particle size
    C. surface seal coats
    D. slurry seals with voids

17. Fine-graded asphalt concrete and hot sand asphalt are quiet riding and are also   17.____

    A. recommended for low traffic pavements
    B. used as slurry seal coats
    C. suitable for major leveling
    D. exceptionally pleasing in appearance

18. The materials that may fulfill surface requirements for low traffic pavements are   18.____

    A. fine-graded asphalt concretes
    B. hot sand asphalts
    C. seal coats or slurry seals
    D. those that can be used for minor leveling

Questions 19-25.

DIRECTIONS: Questions 19 through 25 are to be answered SOLELY on the basis of the paragraphs below.

OPEN-END WRENCHES

Solid, non-adjustable wrenches with openings in one or both ends are called open-end wrenches. Wrenches with small openings are usually shorter than wrenches with large openings. This proportions the lever advantage of the wrench to the bolt or stud and helps prevent wrench breakage or damage to the bolt or stud.

Open-end wrenches may have their jaws parallel to the handle or at angles anywhere up to 90 degrees. The average angle is 15 degrees. This angular displacement variation permits selection of a wrench suited for places where there is room to make only a part of a complete turn of a nut or bolt. Handles are usually straight, but may be curved. Those with curved handles are called S-wrenches. Other open-end wrenches may have offset handles. This allows the head to reach nut or bolt heads that are sunk below the surface.

There are a few basic rules that you should keep in mind when using wrenches. They are:
    I.   ALWAYS use a wrench that fits the nut properly. Otherwise, the wrench may slip, or the nut may be damaged.
    II.   Keep wrenches clean and free from oil. Otherwise, they may slip, resulting in possible serious injury to you or damage to the work.
    III.   Do NOT increase the leverage of a wrench by placing a pipe over the handle. Increased leverage may damage the wrench or the work.

19. Open-end wrenches   19.____

    A. are adjustable
    B. are solid
    C. always have openings at both ends
    D. are always S-shaped

20. Wrench proportions are such that wrenches with _____ openings have _____ handles.   20.____

    A. larger; shorter   B. smaller; longer
    C. larger; longer   D. smaller; thicker

21. The average angle between the jaws and the handle of a wrench is _____ degrees.   21.____

    A. 0   B. 15   C. 22   D. 90

22. Offset handles are intended for use MAINLY with   22.____

    A. offset nuts
    B. bolts having fine threads
    C. nuts sunk below the surface
    D. bolts that permit limited swing

23. The wrench which is selected should fit the nut properly because this   23.____

    A. prevents distorting the wrench
    B. insures use of all wrench sizes
    C. avoids damaging the nut
    D. overstresses the bolt

24. Oil on wrenches is   24.____

    A. *good* because it prevents rust
    B. *good* because it permits easier turning
    C. *bad* because the wrench may slip off the nut
    D. *bad* because the oil may spoil the work

25. Extending the handle of a wrench by slipping a piece of pipe over it is considered   25.____

    A. *good* because it insures a tight nut
    B. *good* because less effort is needed to loosen a nut
    C. *bad* because the wrench may be damaged
    D. *bad* because the amount of tightening can not be controlled

---

KEY (CORRECT ANSWERS)

1. D	11. C
2. B	12. A
3. B	13. B
4. C	14. C
5. D	15. B
6. C	16. A
7. C	17. D
8. B	18. C
9. A	19. B
10. D	20. C

21. B
22. C
23. C
24. C
25. C

TEST 2

DIRECTIONS: Each question or incomplete statement is followed by several suggested answers or completions. Select the one that BEST answers the question or completes the statement. *PRINT THE LETTER OF THE CORRECT ANSWER IN THE SPACE AT THE RIGHT.*

Questions 1-3.

DIRECTIONS: Questions 1 through 3 are to be answered SOLELY on the basis of the following passage.

A utility plan is a floor plan which shows the layout of a heating, electrical, plumbing, or other utility system. Utility plans are used primarily by the persons reponsible for the utilities, but they are important to the craftsman as well. Most utility installations require the leaving of openings in walls, floors, and roofs for the admission or installation of utility features. The craftsman who is, for example, pouring a concrete foundation wall must study the utility plans to determine the number, sizes, and locations of the openings he must leave for piping, electric lines, and the like.

1. The one of the following items of information which is LEAST likely to be provided by a utility plan is the   1.____

   A. location of the joists and frame members around stairwells
   B. location of the hot water supply and return piping
   C. location of light fixtures
   D. number of openings in the floor for radiators

2. According to the passage, the persons who will *most likely* have the GREATEST need for the information included in a utility plan of a building are those who   2.____

   A. maintain and repair the heating system
   B. clean the premises
   C. paint housing exteriors
   D. advertise property for sale

3. According to the passage, a repair crew member should find it MOST helpful to consult a utility plan when information is needed about the   3.____

   A. thickness of all doors in the structure
   B. number of electrical outlets located throughout the structure
   C. dimensions of each window in the structure
   D. length of a roof rafter

Questions 4-9.

DIRECTIONS: Questions 4 through 9 are to be answered SOLELY on the basis of the following passage.

The basic hand-operated hoisting device is the tackle or purchase, consisting of a line called a fall, reeved through one or more blocks. To hoist a load of given size, you must set up a rig with a safe working load equal to or in excess of the load to be hoisted. In order to do this, you must be able to calculate the safe working load of a single part of line of given size, the safe working load of a given purchase which contains a line of given size, and the minimum size of hooks or shackles which you must use in a given type of purchase to hoist a given load. You must also be able to calculate the thrust which a given load will exert on a gin pole or a set of shears inclined at a given angle, the safe working load which a spar of a given size used as a gin pole or as one of a set of shears will sustain, and the stress which a given load will set up in the back guy of a gin pole or in the back guy of a set of shears inclined at a given angle.

4. The above passage refers to the lifting of loads by means of 4.____

    A. erected scaffolds   B. manual rigging devices
    C. power-driven equipment   D. conveyor belts

5. It can be concluded from the above passage that a set of shears serves to 5.____

    A. absorb the force and stress of the working load
    B. operate the tackle
    C. contain the working load
    D. compute the safe working load

6. According to the above passage, a spar can be used for a 6.____

    A. back guy   B. block   C. fall   D. gin pole

7. According to the above passage, the rule that a user of hand-operated tackle MUST follow is to make sure that the safe working load is AT LEAST 7.____

    A. equal to the weight of the given load
    B. twice the combined weight of the block and falls
    C. one-half the weight of the given load
    D. twice the weight of the given load

8. According to the above passage, the two parts that make up a tackle are 8.____

    A. back guys and gin poles   B. blocks and falls
    C. rigs and shears   D. spars and shackles

9. According to the above passage, in order to determine whether it is safe to hoist a particular load, you MUST 9.____

    A. use the maximum size hooks
    B. time the speed to bring a given load to a desired place
    C. calculate the forces exerted on various types of rigs
    D. repeatedly lift and lower various loads

Questions 10-15.

DIRECTIONS: Questions 10 through 15 are to be answered SOLELY on the basis of the following set of instructions.

PATCHING SIMPLE CRACKS IN A BUILT-UP ROOF

If there is a visible crack in built-up roofing, the repair is simple and straightforward:

1. With a brush, clean all loose gravel and dust out of the crack, and clean three or four inches around all sides of it.
2. With a trowel or putty knife, fill the crack with asphalt cement and then spread a layer of asphalt cement about 1/8 inch thick over the cleaned area.
3. Place a strip of roofing felt big enough to cover the crack into the wet cement and press it down firmly.
4. Spread a second layer of cement over the strip of felt and well past its edges.
5. Brush gravel back over the patch.

10. According to the above passage, in order to patch simple cracks in a built-up roof, it is necessary to use a

   A. putty knife and a drill
   B. knife and pliers
   C. tack hammer and a punch
   D. brush and a trowel

10.____

11. According to the above passage, the size of the area that should be clear of loose gravel and dust before the asphalt cement is first applied should

   A. be the exact size of the crack itself
   B. extend three or four inches on all sides of the crack
   C. be 1/8 inch greater than the size of the crack itself
   D. extend the length of the roofing strip

11.____

12. According to the above passage, loose gravel and dust in the crack should be removed with a

   A. brush   B. felt pad   C. trowel   D. dust mop

12.____

13. Assume that both layers of asphalt cement needed to patch the crack are of the same thickness.
    The total thickness of asphalt cement used in the patch should be MOST NEARLY _____ inch.

   A. 1/2   B. 1/3   C. 1/4   D. 1/8

13.____

14. According to the instructions in the above passage, how large should the strip of roofing felt be cut?

   A. Three of four inches square
   B. Smaller than the crack and small enough to be surrounded by cement on all sides of the strip
   C. Exactly the same size and shape of the area covered by the wet cement
   D. Large enough to completely cover the crack

14.____

15. The final or finishing action to be taken in patching a simple crack in a built-up roof is to

   A. clean out the inside of the crack
   B. spread a layer of asphalt a second time
   C. cover the crack with roofing felt
   D. cover the patch of roofing felt and cement with gravel

15.____

Questions 16-17.

DIRECTIONS: Questions 16 and 17 are to be answered SOLELY on the basis of the information given in the following paragraph.

Supplies are to be ordered from the stockroom once a week. The standard requisition
form, Form SP21, is to be used for ordering all supplies. The form is prepared in triplicate,
one white original and two green copies. The white and one green copy are sent to the stockroom, and the remaining green copy is to be kept by the orderer until the supplies are
received.

16.   According to the above paragraph, there is a limit on the   16.____

    A.   amount of supplies that may be ordered
    B.   day on which supplies may be ordered
    C.   different kinds of supplies that may be ordered
    D.   number of times supplies may be ordered in one year

17.   According to the above paragraph, when the standard requisition form for supplies is pre-   17.____
pared,

    A.   a total of four requisition blanks is used
    B.   a white form is the original
    C.   each copy is printed in two colors
    D.   one copy is kept by the stock clerk

Questions 18-21.

DIRECTION: Questions 18 through 21 are to be answered SOLELY on the basis of the following passage.

The Oil Pollution Act for U. S. waters defines an *oily mixture* as 100 parts or more of oil in
one million parts of mixture. This mixture is not allowed to be discharged into the prohibited
zone. The prohibited zone may, in special cases, be extended 100 miles out to sea but, in
general, remains at 50 miles offshore. The United States Coast Guard must be contacted to
report all *oily mixture* spills. The Federal Water Pollution Control Act provides for a fine of
$10,000 for failure to notify the United States Coast Guard. An employer may take action
against an employee if the employee causes an *oily mixture* spill. The law holds your
employer responsible for either cleaning up or paying for the removal of the oil spillage.

18.   According to the Oil Pollution Act, an *oily mixture* is defined as one in which there are   18.____
_____ parts or more of oil in _____ parts of mixture.

    A.   50; 10,000   B.   100; 10,000
    C.   100; 1,000,000   D.   10,000; 1,000,000

19.   Failure to notify the proper authorities of an *oily mixture* spill is punishable by a fine. Such   19.____
fine is provided for by the

    A.   United States Coast Guard
    B.   Federal Water Pollution Control Act
    C.   Oil Pollution Act
    D.   United States Department of Environmental Protection

20. According to the law, the one responsible for the removal of an *oily mixture* spilled into U.S. waters is the   20.____

    A. employer
    B. employee
    C. U.S. Coast Guard
    D. U.S. Pollution Control Board

21. The *prohibited zone,* in general, is the body of water   21.____

    A. within 50 miles offshore
    B. beyond 100 miles offshore
    C. within 10,000 yards of the coastline
    D. beyond 10,000 yards from the coastline

Questions 22-25.

DIRECTIONS: Questions 22 through 25 are to be answered SOLELY on the basis of the following paragraph.

Synthetic detergents are materials produced from petroleum products or from animal or vegetable oils and fats. One of their advantages is the fact that they can be made to meet a particular cleaning problem by altering the foaming, wetting, and emulsifying properties of a cleaner. They are added to commonly used cleaning materials such as solvents, water, and alkalies to improve their cleaning performance. The adequate wetting of the surface to be cleaned is paramount in good cleaning performance. Because of the relatively high surface tension of water, it has poor wetting ability, unless its surface tension is decreased by addition of a detergent or soap. This allows water to flow into crevices and around small particles of soil, thus loosening them.

22. According to the above paragraph, synthetic detergents are made from all of the following EXCEPT   22.____

    A. petroleum products   B. vegetable oils
    C. surface tension oils   D. animal fats

23. According to the above paragraph, water's poor wetting ability is related to   23.____

    A. its low surface tension
    B. its high surface tension
    C. its vegetable oil content
    D. the amount of dirt on the surface to be cleaned

24. According to the above paragraph, synthetic detergents are added to all of the following EXCEPT   24.____

    A. alkalines   B. water   C. acids   D. solvents

25. According to the above paragraph, altering a property of a cleaner can give an advan-   25.____
tage in meeting a certain cleaning problem.
The one of the following that is NOT a property altered by synthetic detergents is the
cleaner's

   A. flow ability   B. foaming property
   C. emulsifying property   D. wetting ability

KEY (CORRECT ANSWERS)

1.	A		11.	B
2.	A		12.	A
3.	B		13.	C
4.	B		14.	D
5.	A		15.	D
6.	D		16.	D
7.	A		17.	B
8.	B		18.	C
9.	C		19.	B
10.	D		20.	A

21.	A
22.	C
23.	B
24.	C
25.	A

READING COMPREHENSION
UNDERSTANDING AND INTERPRETING WRITTEN MATERIAL
EXAMINATION SECTION
TEST 1

DIRECTIONS: Each question or incomplete statement is followed by several suggested answers or completions. Select the one that BEST answers the question or completes the statement. *PRINT THE LETTER OF THE CORRECT ANSWER IN THE SPACE AT THE RIGHT.*

Questions 1-2.

DIRECTIONS: Questions 1 and 2 are to be answered SOLELY on the basis of the following paragraph.

When fixing an upper sash cord, you must also remove the lower sash. To do this, the parting strip between the sash must be removed. Now remove the cover from the weight box channel, cut off the cord as before, and pull it over the pulleys. Pull your new cord over the pulleys and down into the channel where it may be fastened to the weight. The cord for an upper sash is cut off 1" or 2" below the pulley with the weight resting on the floor of the pocket and the cord held taut. These measurements allow for slight stretching of the cord. When the cord is cut to length, it can be pulled up over the pulley and tied with a single common knot in the end to fit into the socket in the sash groove. If the knot protrudes beyond the face of the sash, tap it gently to flatten. In this way, it will not become frayed from constant rubbing against the groove.

1. When repairing the upper sash cord, the FIRST thing to do is to
    A. remove the lower sash
    B. cut the existing sash cord
    C. remove the parting strip
    D. measure the length of new cord necessary

1._____

2. According to the above paragraph, the rope may become frayed if the
    A. pulley is too small   B. knot sticks out
    C. cord is too long   D. weight is too heavy

2._____

Questions 3-4.

DIRECTIONS: Questions 3 and 4 are to be answered SOLELY on the basis of the following paragraph.

Repeated burning of the same area should be avoided. Burning should not be done on impervious, shallow, unstable, or highly erodible soils, or on steep slopes—especially in areas subject to heavy rains or rapid snowmelt. When existing vegetation is likely to be killed or seriously weakened by the fire, measures should be taken to assure prompt revegetation of the burned area. Burns should be limited to relatively small proportions of a watershed unit so that the stream channels will be able to carry any increased flows with a minimum of damage.

3. According to the above paragraph, planned burning should be limited to small areas of the watershed because

    A.   the fire can be better controlled
    B.   existing vegetation will be less likely to be killed
    C.   plants will grow quicker in small areas
    D.   there will be less likelihood of damaging floods

3._____

4. According to the above paragraph, burning USUALLY should be done on soils that

    A.   readily absorb moisture
    B.   have been burnt before
    C.   exist as a thin layer over rock
    D.   can be flooded by nearby streams

4._____

Questions 5-11.

DIRECTIONS: Questions 5 through 11 are to be answered SOLELY on the basis of the following paragraph.

FUSE INFORMATION

Badly bent or distorted fuse clips cannot be permitted. Sometimes, the distortion or bending is so slight that it escapes notice, yet it may be the cause for fuse failures through the heat that is developed by the poor contact. Occasionally, the proper spring tension of the fuse clips has been destroyed by overheating from loose wire connections to the clips. Proper contact surfaces must be maintained to avoid faulty operation of the fuse. Maintenance men should remove oxides that form on the copper and brass contacts, check the clip pressure, and make sure that contact surfaces are not deformed or bent in any way. When removing oxides, use a well-worn file and remove only the oxide film. Do not use sandpaper or emery cloth as hard particles may come off and become embedded in the contact surfaces. All wire connections to the fuse holders should be carefully inspected to see that they are tight.

5. Fuse failure because of poor clip contact or loose connections is due to the resulting

    A.   excessive voltage   B.   increased current
    C.   lowered resistance   D.   heating effect

5._____

6. Oxides should be removed from fuse contacts by using

    A.   a dull file   B.   emery cloth
    C.   fine sandpaper   D.   a sharp file

6._____

7. One result of loose wire connections at the terminal of a fuse clip is stated in the above paragraph to be

    A.   loss of tension in the wire
    B.   welding of the fuse to the clip
    C.   distortion of the clip
    D.   loss of tension of the clip

7._____

8. Simple reasoning will show that the oxide film referred to is undesirable CHIEFLY because it 8._____
    A. looks dull
    B. makes removal of the fuse difficult
    C. weakens the clips
    D. introduces undesirable resistance

9. Fuse clips that are bent very slightly 9._____
    A. should be replaced with new clips
    B. should be carefully filed
    C. may result in blowing of the fuse
    D. may prevent the fuse from blowing

10. From the fuse information paragraph, it would be reasonable to conclude that fuse clips 10._____
    A. are difficult to maintain
    B. must be given proper maintenance
    C. require more attention than other electrical equipment
    D. are unreliable

11. A safe practical way of checking the tightness of the wire connection to the fuse clips of a live 120-volt lighting circuit is to 11._____
    A. feel the connection with your hand to see if it is warm
    B. try tightening with an insulated screwdriver or socket wrench
    C. see if the circuit works
    D. measure the resistance with an ohmmeter

Questions 12-13.

DIRECTIONS: Questions 12 through 13 are to be answered SOLELY on the basis of the following paragraph.

For cast iron pipe lines, the middle ring or sleeve shall have *beveled* ends and shall be high quality cast iron. The middle ring shall have a minimum wall thickness of 3/8" for pipe up to 8", 7/16" for pipe 10" to 30", and 1/2" for pipe over 30", nominal diameter. Minimum length of middle ring shall be 5" for pipe up to 10", 6" for pipe 10" to 30", and 10" for pipe 30" nominal diameter and larger. The middle ring shall not have a center pipe stop, unless otherwise specified.

12. As used in the above paragraph, the word *beveled* means MOST NEARLY 12._____
    A. straight   B. slanted   C. curved   D. rounded

13. In accordance with the above paragraph, the middle ring of a 24" nominal diameter pipe would have a minimum wall thickness and length of _____ thick and _____ long. 13._____
    A. 3/8"; 5:   B. 3/8"; 6"
    C. 7/16"; 6"   D. 1/2"; 6"

Questions 14-17.

DIRECTIONS: Questions 14 through 17 are to be answered SOLELY on the basis of the following paragraph.

Operators spotting loads with long booms and working around men need the smooth, easy operation and positive control of uniform pressure swing clutches. There are no jerks or grabs with these large disc-type clutches because there is always even pressure over the entire clutch lining surface. In the conventional band-type swing clutch, the pressure varies between dead and live ends of the band. The uniform pressure swing clutch has excellent provision for heat dissipation. The driving elements, which are always rotating, have a great number of fins cast in them. This gives them an impeller or blower action for cooling, resulting in longer life and freedom from frequent adjustment.

14. According to the above paragraph, it may be said that conventional band-type swing clutches have   14._____
    A. even pressure on the clutch lining
    B. larger contact area
    C. smaller contact area
    D. uneven pressure on the clutch lining

15. According to the above paragraph, machines equipped with uniform pressure swing clutches will   15._____
    A. give better service under all conditions
    B. require no clutch adjustment
    C. give positive control of hoist
    D. provide better control of swing

16. According to the above paragraph, it may be said that the rotation of the driving elements of the uniform pressure swing clutch is ALWAYS   16._____
    A. continuous   B. constant
    C. varying   D. uncertain

17. According to the above paragraph, freedom from frequent adjustment is due to the   17._____
    A. operator's smooth, easy operation
    B. positive control of the clutch
    C. cooling effect of the rotating fins
    D. larger contact area of the bigger clutch

Questions 18-22.

DIRECTIONS: Questions 18 through 22 are to be answered SOLELY on the basis of the following paragraphs.

Exhaust valve clearance adjustment on diesel engines is very important for proper operation of the engine. Insufficient clearance between the exhaust valve stem and the rocker arm causes a loss of compression and, after a while, burning of the valves and valve seat inserts. On the other hand, too much valve clearance will result in noisy operation of the engine.

Exhaust valves that are maintained in good operating condition will result in efficient combustion in the engine. Valve seats must be true and unpitted, and valve stems must work smoothly within the valve guides. Long valve life will result from proper maintenance and operation of the engine.

Engine operating temperatures should be maintained between 160°F and 185°F. Low operating temperatures result in incompl ete combustion and the deposit of fuel lacquers on valves.

18. According to the above paragraphs, too much valve clearance will cause the engine to operate   18._____
     A. slowly   B. noisily   C. smoothly   D. cold

19. On the basis of the information given in the above paragraphs, operating temperatures of a diesel engine should be between   19._____
     A. 125°F and 130°F   B. 140°F and 150°F
     C. 160°F and 185°F   D. 190°F and 205°F

20. According to the above paragraphs, the deposit of fuel lacquers on valves is caused by   20._____
     A. high operating temperatures
     B. insufficient valve clearance
     C. low operating temperatures
     D. efficient combustion

21. According to the above paragraphs, for efficient operation of the engine, valve seats must   21._____
     A. have sufficient clearance
     B. be true and unpitted
     C. operate at low temperatures
     D. be adjusted regularly

22. According to the above paragraphs, a loss of compression is due to insufficient clearance between the exhaust valve stem and the   22._____
     A. rocker arm   B. valve seat
     C. valve seat inserts   D. valve guides

Questions 23-25.

DIRECTIONS: Questions 23 through 25 are to be answered SOLELY on the basis of the following excerpt:

A SPECIFICATION FOR ELECTRIC WORK FOR THE CITY

Breakers shall be equipped with magnetic blowout coils...Handles of breakers shall be trip-free...Breakers shall be designed to carry 100% of trip rating continuously; to have inverse time delay tripping above 100% of trip rating...

23. According to the above paragraph, the breaker shall have provision for   23._____
     A. resetting   B. arc quenching
     C. adjusting trip time   D. adjusting trip rating

24. According to the above paragraph, the breaker   24._____
     A. shall trip easily at exactly 100% of trip rating
     B. shall trip instantly at a little more than 100% of trip rating
     C. should be constructed so that it shall not be possible to prevent it from opening on overload or short circuit by holding the handle in the ON position
     D. shall not trip prematurely at 100% of trip rating

25. According to the above paragraph, the breaker shall trip   25._____
    A.   instantaneously as soon as 100% of trip rating is reached
    B.   instantaneously as soon as 100% of trip rating is exceeded
    C.   more quickly the greater the current, once 100% of trip rating is exceeded
    D.   after a predetermined fixed time lapse, once 100% of trip rating is reached

_____

KEY (CORRECT ANSWERS)

1.	C	11.	B
2.	B	12.	B
3.	D	13.	C
4.	A	14.	D
5.	D	15.	D
6.	A	16.	A
7.	D	17.	C
8.	D	18.	B
9.	C	19.	C
10.	B	20.	C

21.	B
22.	A
23.	B
24.	C
25.	C

_____

TEST 2

DIRECTIONS: Each question or incomplete statement is followed by several suggested answers or completions. Select the one that BEST answers the question or completes the statement. *PRINT THE LETTER OF THE CORRECT ANSWER IN THE SPACE AT THE RIGHT.*

Questions 1-4.

DIRECTIONS: Questions 1 through 4 are to be answered SOLELY on the basis of the following paragraph.

A low pressure hot water boiler shall include a relief valve or valves of a capacity such that with the heat generating equipment operating at maximum, the pressure cannot rise more than 20 percent above the maximum allowable working pressure (set pressure) if that is 30 p.s.i. gage or less, nor more than 10 percent if it is more than 30 p.s.i. gage. The difference between the set pressure and the pressure at which the valve is relieving is known as *over-pressure or accumulation*. If the steam relieving capacity in pounds per hour is calculated, it shall be determined by dividing by 1,000 the maximum BTU output at the boiler nozzle obtainable from the heat generating equipment, or by multiplying the square feet of heating surface by five.

1. In accordance with the above paragraph, the capacity of a relief valve should be computed on the basis of   1._____
   A. size of boiler
   B. maximum rated capacity of generating equipment
   C. average output of the generating equipment
   D. minimum capacity of generating equipment

2. In accordance with the above paragraph, with a set pressure of 30 p.s.i. gage, the overpressure should not be more than _____ p.s.i.   2._____
   A. 3   B. 6   C. 33   D. 36

3. In accordance with the above paragraph, a relief valve should start relieving at a pressure equal to the   3._____
   A. set pressure
   B. over pressure
   C. over pressure minus set pressure
   D. set pressure plus over pressure

4. In accordance with the above paragraph, the steam relieving capacity can be computed by   4._____
   A. *multiplying* the maximum BTU output by 5
   B. *dividing* the pounds of steam per hour by 1,000
   C. *dividing* the maximum BTU output by the square feet of heating surface
   D. *dividing* the maximum BTU output by 1,000

Questions 5-8.

DIRECTIONS: Questions 5 through 8 are to be answered SOLELY on the basis of the following paragraph.

Air conditioning units requiring a minimum rate of flow of water in excess of one-half (1/2) gallon per minute shall be metered. Air conditioning equipment with a refrigeration unit which has a definite rate of capacity in tons or fractions thereof, the charge will be at the rate of $30 per annum per ton capacity from the date installed to the date when the supply is metered. Such units, when equipped with an approved water-conserving device, shall be charged at the rate of $4.50 per annum per ton capacity from the date installed to the date when the supply is metered.

5. A man who was in the market for air conditioning equipment was considering three different units. Unit 1 required a flow of 28 gallons of water per hour; Unit 2 required 30 gallons of water per hour; Unit 3 required 32 gallons of water per hour. The man asked the salesman which units would require the installation of a water meter. According to the above passage, the salesman SHOULD answer:
    A.   All three units require meters
    B.   Units 2 and 3 require meters
    C.   Unit 3 only requires a meter
    D.   None of the units require a meter
5._____

6. Suppose that air conditioning equipment with a refrigeration unit of 10 tons was put in operation on October 1; and in the following year on July 1, a meter was installed. According to the above passage, the charge for this period would be _____ the annual rate.
    A.   twice   B.   equal to
    C.   three-fourths   D.   one-fourth
6._____

7. The charge for air conditioning equipment which has no refrigeration unit
    A.   is $30 per year
    B.   is $25.50 per year
    C.   is $4.50 per year
    D.   cannot be determined from the above passage
7._____

8. The charge for air conditioning equipment with a seven-ton refrigeration unit equipped with an approved water-conserving device
    A.   is $4.50 per year
    B.   is $25.50 per year
    C.   is $31.50 per year
    D.   cannot be determined from the above passage
8._____

Questions 9-14.

DIRECTIONS: Questions 9 through 14 are to be answered SOLELY on the basis of the following paragraph.

The city makes unremitting efforts to keep the water free from pollution. An inspectional force under a sanitary expert is engaged in patrolling the watersheds to see that the department's sanitary regulations are observed. Samples taken daily from various points in the water supply system are examined and analyzed at the three laboratories maintained by the department. All water before delivery to the distribution mains is treated with chlorine to destroy bacteria. In addition, some water is aerated to free it from gases and, in some cases, from microscopic organisms. Generally, microscopic organisms which develop in the reservoirs and at times impart an unpleasant taste and odor to the water, though in no sense harmful to health, are destroyed by treatment with copper sulfate and by chlorine dosage. None of the supplies is filtered, but the quality of the water supplied by the city is excellent for all purposes, and it is clear and wholesome.

9. According to the above paragraph, microscopic organisms are removed from   9._____
    the water supplied to the city by means of
    A. chlorine alone
    B. chlorine, aeration, and filtration
    C. chlorine, aeration, filtration, and sampling
    D. copper sulfate, chlorine, and aeration

10. Microscopic organisms in the water supply GENERALLY are   10._____
    A. a health menace   B. impossible to detect
    C. not harmful to health   D. not destroyed in the water

11. The MAIN function of the inspectional force, as described in the above   11._____
    paragraph, is to
    A. take samples of water for analysis
    B. enforce sanitary regulations
    C. add chlorine to the water supply
    D. inspect water-use meters

12. According to the above paragraph, chlorine is added to water before entering   12._____
    the
    A. watersheds   B. reservoirs
    C. distribution mains   D. run-off areas

13. Of the following suggested headings or titles for the above paragraph, the one   13._____
    that BEST tells what the paragraph is about is
    A. QUALITY OF WATER   B. CHLORINATION OF WATER
    C. TESTING OF WATER   D. BACTERIA IN WATER

14. The MOST likely reason for taking samples of water for examination and   14._____
    analysis from various points in the water supply system is:
    A. The testing points are convenient to the department's laboratories
    B. Water from one part of the system may be made undrinkable by a
        local condition
    C. The samples can be distributed equally among the three laboratories
    D. The hardness or softness of water varies from place to place

Questions 15-17.

DIRECTIONS: Questions 15 through 17 are to be answered SOLELY on the basis
                of the following paragraph.

A building measuring 200' x 100' at the street is set back 20' on all sides at the 15th floor, and an additional 10' on all sides at the 30th floor. The building is 35 stories high.

15. The **floor area** of the 16th floor is **MOST NEARLY** _____ sq. ft. 15._____
    A. 20,000 B. 14,400 C. 9,600 D. 7,500

16. The floor area of the 35th floor is **MOST NEARLY** _____ sq. ft. 16._____
    A. 20,000 B. 13,900 C. 7,500 D. 5,600

17. The floor area of the 16th floor, compared to the floor area of the 2nd floor, is 17._____
MOST NEARLY _____ as much.
    A. three-fourths (3/4)   B. two-thirds (2/3)
    C. one-half (1/2)   D. four-tenths (4/10)

Question 18.

DIRECTIONS: Question 18 is to be answered SOLELY on the basis of the following paragraph.

Experience has shown that, in general, a result of the installation of meters on services not previously metered is to reduce the amount of water consumed, but is not necessarily to reduce the peak load on plumbing systems. The permissible head loss through meters at their rated maximum flow is 20 p.s.i. The installation of a meter may therefore appreciably lower the pressures available in fixtures on a plumbing system.

18. According to the above paragraph, a water meter may 18._____
    A. limit the flow in the plumbing system of 20 p.s.i.
    B. reduce the peak load on the plumbing system
    C. increase the overall amount of water consumed
    D. reduce the pressure in the plumbing system

Question 19.

DIRECTIONS: Question 19 is to be answered SOLELY on the basis of the following paragraph.

Spring comes without trumpets to a city. The asphalt is a wilderness that does not quicken overnight; winds blow gritty with cinders instead of merry with the smells of earth and fertilizer. Women wear their gardens on their hats. But spring is a season in the city, and it has its own harbingers, constant as daffodils. Shop windows change their colors, people walk more slowly on the streets, what one can see of the sky has a bluer tone. Pulitzer prizes awake and sing and matinee tickets go-a-begging. But gayer than any of these are the carousels, which are already in sheltered places, beginning to turn with the sound of springtime itself. They are the earliest and the truest and the oldest of all the urban signs.

19. In the passage above, the word *harbingers* means 19._____
    A. storms B. truths C. virtues D. forerunners

Questions 20-22.

DIRECTIONS: Questions 20 through 22 are to be answered SOLELY on the basis of the following paragraph.

Gas heaters include manually operated, automatic, and instantaneous heaters. Some heaters are equipped with a thermostat which controls the fuel supply so that when the water falls below a predetermined temperature, the fuel is automatically turned on. In some types, the hot-water storage tank is well-insulated to economize the use of fuel. Instantaneous heaters are arranged so that the opening of a faucet on the hot-water pipe will increase the flow of fuel, which is ignited by a continuously burning pilot light to heat the water to from 120° to 130°F. The possibility that the pilot light will die out offers a source of danger in the use of automatic appliances which depend on a pilot light. Gas and oil heaters are dangerous, and they should be designed to prevent the accumulation, in a confined space within the heater, of a large volume of an explosive mixture.

20. According to the above passage, the opening of a hot-water faucet on a hot-water pipe connected to an instantaneous hot-water heater will the pilot light.　　20._____
    A. *increase* the temperature of
    B. *increase* the flow of fuel to
    C. *decrease* the flow of fuel to
    D. *have a marked effect* on

21. According to the above passage, the fuel is automatically turned on in a heater equipped with a thermostat whenever　　21._____
    A. the water temperature drops below 120°F
    B. the pilot light is lit
    C. the water temperature drops below some predetermined temperature
    D. a hot water supply is opened

22. According to the above passage, some hot-water storage tanks are well-insulated to　　22._____
    A. accelerate the burning of the fuel
    B. maintain the water temperature between 120° and 130°F
    C. prevent the pilot light from being extinguished
    D. minimize the expenditure of fuel

Question 23.

DIRECTIONS: Question 23 is to be answered SOLELY on the basis of the following paragraph.

Breakage of the piston under high-speed operation has been the commonest fault of disc piston meters. Various techniques are adopted to prevent this, such as *throttling* the meter, cutting away the edge of the piston, or reinforcing it, but these are simply makeshifts.

23. As used in the above paragraph, the word *throttling* means MOST NEARLY　　23._____
    A. enlarging   B. choking
    C. harnessing   D. dismantling

Questions 24-25.

DIRECTIONS: Questions 24 and 25 are to be answered SOLELY on the basis of the following paragraph.

One of the most common and objectionable difficulties occurring in a drainage system is trap seal loss. This failure can be attributed directly to inadequate ventilation of the trap and the subsequent negative and positive pressures which occur. A trap seal may be lost either by siphonage and/or back pressure. Loss of the trap seal by siphonage is the result of a negative pressure in the drainage system. The seal content of the trap is forced by siphonage into the waste piping of the drainage system through exertion of atmospheric pressure on the fixture side of the trap seal.

24. According to the above paragraph, a positive pressure is a direct result of   24._____
    A. siphonage   B. unbalanced trap seal
    C. poor ventilation   D. atmospheric pressure

25. According to the above paragraph, the water in the trap is forced into the drain   25._____
    pipe by
    A. atmospheric pressure   B. back pressure
    C. negative pressure   D. back pressure on fixture side of seal

_____

KEY (CORRECT ANSWERS)

1.	B	11.	B
2.	B	12.	C
3.	D	13.	A
4.	D	14.	B
5.	C	15.	C
6.	C	16.	D
7.	D	17.	C
8.	C	18.	D
9.	D	19.	B
10.	C	20.	B

21.	C
22.	D
23.	B
24.	C
25.	A

_____

READING COMPREHENSION
UNDERSTANDING AND INTERPRETING WRITTEN MATERIAL
EXAMINATION SECTION
TEST 1

Questions 1-22.

DIRECTIONS: Each question or incomplete statement is followed by several suggested answers or completions. Select the one that BEST answers the question or completes the statement. *PRINT THE LETTER OF THE CORRECT ANSWER IN THE SPACE AT THE RIGHT.*

Questions 1-2.

DIRECTIONS: Questions 1 and 2 are to be answered in accordance with the following paragraph.

    Steam cleaners get their name from the fact that steam is used to generate pressure and is also a by-product of heating the cleaning solution. Steam itself has little cleaning power. It will melt some soils, but it does not dissolve them, break them up, or destroy their clinging power. Rather surprisingly, good machines generate as little steam as possible. Modern surface chemistry depends on a chemical solution to dissolve dirt, destroy its clinging power, and hold it in suspension. Steam actually hinders such a solution, but heat helps its physical and chemical action. Cleaning is most efficient when a hot solution reaches the work in heavy volume.

1. In accordance with the above paragraph, for MOST efficient cleaning,   1.____

    A. a heavy volume of steam is needed
    B. hot steam is needed to break up the soils
    C. steam is used to dissolve the surface dirt
    D. a hot chemical solution should always be used

2. With reference to the above paragraph, the steam in a steam cleaner is used to   2.____

    A. generate pressure
    B. create by-product chemicals
    C. slow down the chemical action of the cleaning solution
    D. dissolve accumulations of dirt

Questions 3-5.

DIRECTIONS: Questions 3 through 5 are based upon the information given in the following paragraphs. Use ONLY the information given in these paragraphs in answering these questions.

METHOD A - Move voltmeter lead from *BAT* to *GEN* terminal of regulator. Retard generator speed until generator voltage is reduced to 2 volts on a 6-volt system or 4 volts on a 12-volt system. Move voltmeter lead back to *BAT* terminal of regulator. Bring generator back to specified speed and note voltage setting.

METHOD B - Connect a variable resistance into the field circuit. Turn out all resistance. Operate generator at specified speed. Slowly increase (turn in) resistance until generator voltage is reduced to 2 volts on a 6-volt system or 4 volts on a 12-volt system. Turn out all resistance again, and note voltage setting. Regulator cover must be in place. To adjust voltage setting, turn adjusting screw. Turn clockwise to increase setting and counterclockwise to decrease voltage setting.

3. According to the instructions given in the paragraphs, when taking readings,   3._____

    A.   a variable resistance is to be connected into the generator armature circuit
    B.   the generator voltage on a 12-volt system is reduced to 2 volts
    C.   the cover is to be in place
    D.   the voltmeter lead should be continuously connected to the *BAT* terminal

4. In following the instructions given in the paragraphs, the one of the following statements   4._____
that is MOST nearly correct is:

    A.   The adjusting screw must be turned clockwise to increase the voltage setting
    B.   Method B makes use of a fixed resistor
    C.   Method A makes use of a variable resistor
    D.   The generator voltage is reduced by decreasing the resistance

5. The above instructions pertain MOST likely to a(n)   5._____

    A.   voltage regulator   B.   starting regulator
    C.   amperage regulator   D.   circuit breaker

Questions 6-7.

DIRECTIONS: Questions 6 and 7 are based upon the following paragraph. Use ONLY the information contained in this paragraph in answering these questions.

With the engine running at normal idling speed and the engine hood open, attach the vacuum gauge to the intake manifold. The vacuum gauge should read about 18 to 21 inches, and the pointer should be steady. A needle fluctuating between 10 and 15 inches may indicate a defective cylinder-head, gasket, or valve. An extremely low reading indicates a leak in the intake manifold or gaskets. Accelerate the engine with full throttle momentarily. Notice if the gauge indicator fails to drop to approximately 2 inches as the throttle is opened, and recoil to at least 24 inches as the throttle is closed. If so, this may be an indication of diluted oil, poor piston-ring sealing, or an abnormal restriction in the exhaust, carburetor, or air cleaner. The above readings apply to sea level. There will be approximately a 1-inch drop for each 1,000 feet of altitude.

6. If a vacuum test is made on a properly operating engine at an altitude of 3,000 feet, the   6._____
vacuum gauge should read MOST NEARLY

    A.   12"   B.   15"   C.   13"   D.   24"

7. If a vacuum test is made on an engine which has an abnormal restriction in the exhaust,   7._____
this will be evidenced by

    A.   a leak in the intake manifold
    B.   the gauge indicator failing to drop to approximately 3 inches on opening the throttle

    C. the gauge fluctuating around 12 inches
    D. a steady high gauge reading

Questions 8-10.

DIRECTIONS: Questions 8 through 10 are to be answered in accordance with the information in the following paragraph.

The following is a set of instructions on engine shut-down procedure: When an engine equipped with an electric shut-down valve is used, the engine can be shut down completely by turning off the switch key on installations equipped with an electric shut-down valve, or by turning the manual shut-down valve lever. Turning off the switch key which controls the electric shut-down valve always stops the engine unless the override button on the shutdown valve has been locked in the open position. If the manual override on the electric shut-down valve is being used, turn the button full counterclockwise to stop the engine.

CAUTION: Never leave the switch key or the override button in the valve open or run position when the engine is not running. With overhead tanks, this would allow fuel to drain into the cylinders, causing hydraulic lock.

8.   According to the above paragraph, it becomes apparent that if an engine does not stop when the electric shut-down valve switch key is shut off,   8._____

    A. an open manual switch is present
    B. the override button is locked in the closed position
    C. a closed manual switch is functioning
    D. the override button is locked in the open position

9.   When using an engine equipped with an electric shut-down valve,   9._____

    A. no alternate method is available
    B. a manual method is not present
    C. a manual override can shut the engine down
    D. a manual override will not work

10.   As a matter of caution, the switch key in the closed position or the override button in the stop position will   10._____

    A. assist in keeping fuel in the cylinders
    B. prevent fuel from flooding the cylinder cavities
    C. assist in producing hydraulic lock
    D. aid fuel dilution

Questions 11-12.

DIRECTIONS: Questions 11 and 12 are to be answered according to the information given in the following paragraph.

You have been instructed to expedite the fabrication of four special salt spreader trucks using chassis that are available in the shop. All four trucks must be delivered before the opening of business on December 1. Based on workload and available hours, the foreman of the body shop indicates that he could manufacture one complete salt spreader body in five weeks, with one additional week required for mounting and securing each body to the available chassis. No work could begin on the body until the engines and hydraulic components, which would have to be purchased, were available for use. The Purchasing Department has promised delivery of engines and hydraulic components three months after the order is placed. (Assume that all months have four weeks, and the same crew is doing the assembling and manufacturing.)

11. With reference to the above paragraph, assuming that the Purchasing Department placed the order at the beginning of the first week in February and ultimate delivery of the engines and components was delayed by six weeks, the date of completion of the first salt spreader truck would be CLOSEST to the end of the _____ week in _____.

   A. fourth; July   B. second; August
   C. fourth; August   D. first; September

11.___

12. With reference to the above paragraph, the LATEST date that the engines and associated hydraulic components could be requisitioned in order to meet the specified deadline would be CLOSEST to the beginning of the _____ week in _____.

   A. first; February   B. first; March
   C. third; March   D. first; April

12.___

Questions 13-20.

DIRECTIONS: Questions 13 through 20 are based on the paragraph on JACKS shown below. When answering these questions, refer to this paragraph.

JACKS

When using a jack, a workman should check the capacity plate or other markings on the jack to make sure the device is heavy enough to support the load. Where there is no plate, capacity should be determined and painted on the side of the jack. The workman should see that jacks are well lubricated, but only at points where lubrication is specified, and should inspect them for broken teeth or faulty holding fixtures. A jack should never be thrown or dropped upon the floor; such treatment may crack or distort the metal, thus causing the jack to break when a load is lifted. It is important that the floor or ground surface upon which the jack is placed be level and clean, and the safe limit of floor loading is not exceeded. If the surface is earth, the jack base should be set on heavy wood blocking, preferably hardwood, of sufficient size that the blocking will not turn over, shift, or sink. If the surface is not perfectly level, the jack may be set on blocking, which should be leveled by wedges securely placed so that they cannot be brushed or forced out of place. *Extenders* of wood or metal, intended to provide a higher rise where a jack cannot reach up to load or lift it high enough, should never be used. Instead, a larger jack should be obtained or higher blocking which is correspondingly wider and longer – should be placed under the jack. All lifts should be vertical with the jack correctly centered for the lift. The base of the jack should be on a perfectly level surface, and the jack head, with its hardwood shim, should bear against a perfectly level meeting surface.

13. To make sure the jack is heavy enough to support a certain load, the workman should

   A. lubricate the jack   B. shim the jack
   C. check the capacity plate   D. use a long handle

13.___

14. A jack should be lubricated   14.____

    A. after using   B. before painting
    C. only at specified points   D. to prevent slipping

15. The workman should inspect a jack for   15.____

    A. manufacturer's name   B. broken teeth
    C. paint peeling   D. broken wedges

16. Metal parts on a jack may crack if   16.____

    A. the jack is thrown on the floor
    B. the load is leveled
    C. blocking is used
    D. the handle is too short

17. It would NOT be a safe practice for a workman to   17.____

    A. center the jack under the load
    B. set the jack on a level surface
    C. use hardwood for blocking
    D. use *extenders* to reach up to the load

18. Wedges may safely be used to   18.____

    A. replace a broken tooth
    B. prevent the overloading of a jack
    C. level the blocking under a jack
    D. straighten distorted metal

19. Blocking should be   19.____

    A. made of a soft wood
    B. placed between the jack base and the earth surface
    C. well lubricated
    D. used to repair a broken tooth

20. A hardwood shim should be used   20.____

    A. between the head and its meeting surface
    B. under the jack
    C. as a filler
    D. to level a surface

Questions 21-22.

DIRECTIONS: Questions 21 and 22 are to be answered ONLY on the basis of the information
                  contained in the following paragraph.

Many experiments have been made on the effects of alcoholic beverages. These studies
show that alcohol decreases alertness and efficiency. It decreases self-consciousness and,
at the same time, increases confidence and feelings of ease and relaxation. It impairs attention and judgment. It destroys fear of consequences. Usual cautions are thrown to the winds.
Habit systems become disorganized. The driver who uses alcohol tends to disregard his

usual safety practices. He may not even be aware that he is disregarding them. His reaction time slows down; normally quick reactions are not possible for him. To make matters worse, he may not realize he is slower. His eye muscles may be so affected that his vision is not normal. He cannot correctly judge the speed of his car or of any other car. He cannot correctly estimate distances being covered by each. He becomes a highway menace.

21. The paragraph states that the drinking of alcohol makes a driver   21.____

    A. *more* alert   B. *less* confident
    C. *more* efficient   D. *less* attentive

22. From the above paragraph, it is reasonable to assume that a driver may overcome the   22.____
bad effects of drinking alcohol by

    A. being more cautious
    B. relying on his good driving habits to a greater extent than normally
    C. watching the road more carefully
    D. waiting for the alcohol to wear off before drinking

Questions 23-25.

DIRECTIONS: Each question consists of a statement. You are to indicate whether the statement is TRUE(T) or FALSE (F). *PRINT THE LETTER OF THE CORRECT ANSWER IN THE SPACE AT THE RIGHT.*

When in use, the storage battery becomes hot, and water evaporates from the cells of the battery, so clean water, preferably distilled, must be added at frequent intervals. This action keeps the level of the battery liquid above the top of the battery plates.

23. All water loss from a storage battery occurs when the battery is in use.   23.____

24. The water added to a storage battery does not have to be distilled.   24.____

25. Water in the storage battery must be kept level with the top of the battery plates.   25.____

KEY (CORRECT ANSWERS)

1.	D		11.	A
2.	A		12.	B
3.	C		13.	C
4.	A		14.	C
5.	A		15.	B
6.	B		16.	A
7.	B		17.	D
8.	D		18.	C
9.	C		19.	B
10.	B		20.	A

21.	D
22.	F
23.	F
24.	T
25.	F

————

TEST 2

DIRECTIONS: Each question or incomplete statement is followed by several suggested answers or completions. Select the one that BEST answers the question or completes the statement. *PRINT THE LETTER OF THE CORRECT ANSWER IN THE SPACE AT THE RIGHT.*

Questions 1-2.

DIRECTIONS: Questions 1 and 2 are based on the following paragraph.

Because electric drills run at high speed, the cutting edges of a twist drill are heated quickly. If the metal is thick, the drill point must be withdrawn from the hole frequently to cool it and clear out chips. Forcing the drill continuously into a deep hole will heat it, thereby spoiling its temper and cutting edges. A portable electric drill has the advantage that it can be taken to the work and used to drill holes in material too large to handle in a drill press.

1. According to the above paragraph, overheating of a twist drill will   1._____

   A. slow down the work
   B. cause excessive drill breakage
   C. dull the drill
   D. spoil the accuracy of the work

2. According to the above paragraph, one method of preventing overheating of a twist drill is   2._____
   to

   A. use cooling oil
   B. drill a smaller pilot hole first
   C. use a drill press
   D. remove the drill from the work frequently

Questions 3-5.

DIRECTIONS: Questions 3 through 5, inclusive, are to be answered in accordance with the paragraph below.

A steam heating system with steam having a pressure of less than 10 pounds is called a low-pressure system. The majority of steam-heating systems are of this type. The steam may be provided by low-pressure boilers installed *expressly* for the purpose, or it may be gener-ated in boilers at a higher pressure and reduced in pressure before admitted to the heating mains. In other instances, it may be possible to use exhaust steam which has been made to run engines and other machines and which still contains enough heat to be utilized in the heating system. The first case represents the system of heating used in the ordinary resi-dence or other small building; the other two represent the systems of heating employed in industrial buildings where a power plant is installed for general power purposes.

3. According to the above paragraph, whether or not a steam heating system is considered   3._____
    a low pressure system is determined by the pressure

    A. generated by the boiler
    B. in the heating main
    C. at the inlet side of the reducing valve
    D. of the exhaust

4. According to the above paragraph, steam used for heating is sometimes obtained from   4._____
    steam

    A. generated principally to operate machinery
    B. exhausted from larger boilers
    C. generated at low pressure and brought up to high pressure before being used
    D. generated by engines other than boilers

5. As used in the above paragraph, the word *expressly* means   5._____

    A. rapidly   B. specifically
    C. usually   D. mainly

Questions 6-7.

DIRECTIONS: Questions 6 and 7 are to be answered in accordance with the paragraph
              below.

    When one is making the selection of grinding wheel specifications, the first variable factor
to consider is the wheel speed, which influences the grade and the bond of the wheel. It is
recommended that the grade should be determined in this way: the higher the wheel speed
with relation to work speed, the softer the wheel should be. When, for any reason, the wheel
speed is reduced, then it may be expected that the wheel will wear faster, but this can be
overcome by choosing a wheel of a harder grade, assuming that the grade was correct for the
initial speed.

6. It can be said that the MOST important piece of information in the above paragraph is: 6._____

    A. The higher the relative wheel speed, the softer should be the wheel
    B. Wheel speed is a variable factor
    C. At low speeds wheels wear rapidly
    D. When a wheel slows down, it should be replaced by a harder grade

7. According to the above paragraph, no indication is made that   7._____

    A. there are other factors to be considered besides speed
    B. hard wheels at low speed wear faster than soft wheels at high speed
    C. the lower the speed the harder should be the grade
    D. the selection of the bond of the wheel is affected by speed

Questions 8-9.

DIRECTIONS: Questions 8 and 9 are to be answered ONLY according to the information in
              the following paragraph.

Metal spraying is used for many purposes. Worn bearings on shafts and spindles can be readily restored to original dimensions with any desired metal or alloy. Low-carbon steel shafts may be supplied with high-carbon steel journal surfaces, which can then be ground to size after spraying. By using babbitt wire, bearings can be lined or babbitted while rotating. Pump shafts and impellers can be coated with any desired metal to overcome wear and corrosion. Valve seats may be re-surfaced. Defective castings can be repaired by filling in blowholes and checks. The application of metal spraying to the field of corrosion resistance is growing, although the major application in this field is in the use of sprayed zinc. Tin, lead, and aluminum have been used considerably. The process is used for structural and tank applications in the field as well as in the shop.

8. According to the above paragraph, worn bearing surfaces on shafts are metal-sprayed in order to

    8.____

    A. prevent corrosion of the shaft
    B. fit them into larger-sized impellers
    C. return them to their original sizes
    D. replace worn babbitt metal

9. According to the above paragraph, rotating bearings can be metal-sprayed using

    9.____

    A. babbitt wire   B. high-carbon steel
    C. low-carbon steel   D. any desired metal

Questions 10-11.

DIRECTIONS: Questions 10 and 11 are to be answered ONLY according to the information in the following paragraph.

The wheels used for internal grinding should generally be softer than those used for other grinding operations because the contact area between the wheel and work is comparatively large. A soft wheel that will cut with little pressure should be used to prevent springing the spindle. The grade of the wheel depends upon the character of the work and the stiffness of the machine; and where a large variety of work is being ground, it may not be practicable to have an assortment of wheels adapted to all conditions. By adjusting the speed, however, a wheel not exactly suited to the work in hand can often be used. If the wheel wears too rapidly, it should be run faster; and if it tends to glaze, the speed should be diminished.

10. On the basis of the above passage only, it may BEST be said that

    10.____

    A. the type and grade of wheel are independent of the sturdiness of the machine
    B. by increasing the wheel speed, parts can easily be internally ground
    C. wheels used for outside grinding usually have a smaller contact area between the wheel and work
    D. to carry on hand an assortment of wheels for all conceivable internal grinding jobs is economical

11. On the basis of the above passage only, it may BEST be said that

    11.____

    A. in general, if a wheel wears too rapidly, the speed should be decreased
    B. by decreasing the wheel speed, a wheel not quite appropriate for the job may sometimes be used

C. where a large variety of work is being ground, the grade of wheel depends on the diameter of the wheel
D. if a wheel tends to glaze, it should run faster

Questions 12-15.

DIRECTIONS: Questions 12 through 15, inclusive, are to be answered ONLY in accordance with the following paragraph.

Cylindrical surfaces are the most common form of finished surfaces found on machine parts, although flat surfaces are also very common; hence, many metal-cutting *processes* are for the purpose of producing either cylindrical or flat surfaces. The machines used for cylindrical or flat shapes may be, and often are, utilized also for forming the various irregular or special shapes required on many machine parts. Because of the prevalence of cylindrical and flat surfaces, the student of manufacturing practice should learn first about the machines and methods employed to produce these surfaces. The cylindrical surfaces may be internal as in holes and cylinders. Any one part may, of course, have cylindrical sections of different diameters and lengths and include flat ends or shoulders; and frequently there is a threaded part or possibly some finished surface that is not circular in cross-section. The prevalence of cylindrical surfaces on machine parts explains why lathes are found in all machine shops. It is important to understand the various uses of the lathe because many of the operations are the same fundamentally as those performed on other types of machine tools.

12. According to the above paragraph, the MOST common form of finished surfaces found on machine parts is

    A. cylindrical
    C. flat
    B. elliptical
    D. square

12.____

13. According to the above paragraph, any one part of cylindrical surfaces may have

    A. chases   B. shoulders   C. keyways   D. splines

13.____

14. According to the above paragraph, lathes are found in all machine shops because cylindrical surfaces on machine parts are

    A. scarce   B. internal   C. common   D. external

14.____

15. As used in the above paragraph, the word *processes* means

    A. operations
    C. devices
    B. purposes
    D. tools

15.____

Questions 16-17.

DIRECTIONS: Questions 16 and 17 are to be answered ONLY in accordance with the following paragraph.

The principle of interchangeability requires manufacture to such specification that component parts of a device may be selected at random and assembled to fit and operate satisfactorily. Interchangeable manufacture, therefore, requires that parts be made to definite limits of error and to fit gages instead of mating parts. Interchangeability does not necessarily involve a high degree of precision; stove lids, for example, are interchangeable but are not particularly accurate, and carriage bolts and nuts are not precision products but are completely interchangeable. Interchangeability may be employed in unit production as well as mass production systems of manufacture.

16. According to the above paragraph, in order for parts to be interchangeable, they must be   16.____

    A. precision-machined   B. selectively-assembled
    C. mass-produced   D. made to fit gages

17. According to the above paragraph, carriage bolts are interchangeable because they are   17.____

    A. precision-made
    B. sized to specific tolerances
    C. individually matched products
    D. produced in small units

Questions 18-22.

DIRECTIONS: Questions 18 through 22 are to be answered in accordance with the following passage.

TITANIC AIR COMPRESSOR

Valves: The compressors are equipped with Titanic plate valves which are automatic in operation. Valves are so constructed that an entire valve assembly can readily be removed from the head. The valves provide large port area with short lift and are accurately guided to insure positive seating.

Starting Unloader: Each compressor (or air end) is equipped with a centrifugal governor which is bolted directly to the compressor crank shaft. The governor actuates cylinder relief valves so as to relieve pressure from the cylinders during starting and stopping. The motor is never required to start the compressor under load.

Air Strainer: Each cylinder air inlet connection is fitted with a suitable combination air strainer and muffler.

Pistons: Pistons are lightweight castings, ribbed internally to secure strength, and are accurately turned and ground. Each piston is fitted with four (4) rings, two of which are oil control rings. Piston pins are hardened and tempered steel of the full floating type. Bronze bushings are used between piston pin and piston.

Connecting Rods: Connecting rods are of solid bronze designed for maximum strength, rigidity, and wear. Crank pins are fitted with renewable steel bushings. Connecting rods are of the one-piece type, there being no bolts, nuts, or cotter pins which can come loose. With this type of construction, wear is reduced to a negligible amount, and adjustment of wrist pin and crank pin bearings is unnecessary.

Main Bearings: Main bearings are of the ball type and are securely held in position by spacers. This type of bearing entirely eliminates the necessity of frequent adjustment or attention. The crank shaft is always in perfect alignment.

Crank Shaft: The crank shaft is a one-piece heat-treated forging of best quality open-hearth steel, of rugged design, and of sufficient size to transmit the motor power and any additional stresses which may occur in service. Each crank shaft is counter-balanced (dynamically balanced) to reduce vibration to a minimum, and is accurately machined to properly receive the ball bearing races, crank pin bushing, flexible coupling, and centrifugal governor. Suitable provision is made to insure proper lubrication of all crank shaft bearings and bushings with the minimum amount of attention.

Coupling: Compressor and motor shafts are connected through a Morse Chain Company all-metal enclosed flexible coupling. This coupling consists of two sprockets, one mounted on, and keyed to, each shaft; the sprockets are wrapped by a single Morse Chain, the entire assembly being enclosed in a split aluminum grease packed cover.

18. The crank pin of the connecting rod is fitted with a renewable bushing made of   18._____

    A. solid bronze   B. steel
    C. slight-weight casting   D. ball bearings

19. When the connecting rod is of the one-piece type,   19._____

    A. the wrist pins require frequent adjustment
    B. the crank pins require frequent adjustment
    C. the cotter pins frequently will come loose
    D. wear is reduced to a negligible amount

20. The centrifugal governor is bolted DIRECTLY to the   20._____

    A. compressor crank shaft   B. main bearing
    C. piston pin   D. muffler

21. The number of oil control rings required for each piston is   21._____

    A. one   B. two   C. three   D. four

22. The compressor and motor shafts are connected through a flexible coupling. These   22._____
couplings are _____ to the shafts.

    A. keyed   B. brazed   C. soldered   D. press fit

Questions 23-25.

DIRECTION: Questions 23 through 25, inclusive, are to be answered in accordance with the following paragraph.

Wherever a soil pipe has to be provided for in a partition, special care must be taken that the hubs do not project beyond the finish face of the plaster. Before framing a building, it is desirable to ascertain where the stacks are and to provide for them. Building regulations require the stacks to be of 4-inch cast-iron even in small dwellings. With a 4-inch stack, the hub is 6 1/8 inches in diameter; and, therefore, 2 by 6 studs must be used. Special care should be taken that no plaster comes in contact with a soil pipe for *subsequent* settlement may cause cracking.

23. As used in the paragraph above, *subsequent* means MOST NEARLY   23._____

    A. heavy   B. sudden   C. later   D. soon

24. According to the above paragraph, 4" cast-iron soil pipes are used because

    A. they will not project beyond the face of the plaster
    B. it is easier to plaster over 4" pipe
    C. they can be located easier
    D. they are required by law

24.____

25. According to the above paragraph, the reason plaster should NOT be in direct contact with soil pipe is because

    A. the plaster would be damaged by moisture
    B. rust will bleed through the plaster
    C. of the possibility of cracks due to settlement
    D. it is harder to plaster over 4" pipe

25.____

KEY (CORRECT ANSWERS)

1.	C		11.	B
2.	D		12.	A
3.	B		13.	B
4.	A		14.	C
5.	B		15.	A
6.	A		16.	D
7.	B		17.	B
8.	C		18.	B
9.	A		19.	D
10.	C		20.	A

21.	B
22.	A
23.	C
24.	D
25.	C
